New Nations and Peoples

West Indies

West Indies

PHILIP SHERLOCK

with 75 illustrations and 3 maps

New York
WALKER AND COMPANY

Library of Congress Catalog Card Number: 66-22506

First published in the United States of America in 1966 by Walker and Company, a division of Publications Development Corporation

Printed in Great Britain

Contents

1   The West Indian Experience

THERE IS NO COUNTRY called the West Indies but there are $3\frac{1}{2}$ million West Indians. The name, like the Antilles, once referred to the Caribbean archipelago; now it is limited to Jamaica, Trinidad and Tobago, Barbados, the Leeward and Windward Islands, whose $3\frac{1}{2}$ million people share with the rest of the Caribbean the experience of colonialism, slavery and the plantation, but whose particular metropolitan association was with Britain. For this reason West Indians are English speaking, and their social and political institutions are patterned after those of England.

History and geography combined in the Caribbean to make an island the symbol of national identity,[1] a country whose frontiers were clearly marked out by the shoreline. The term 'West Indian' extends beyond this limitation, to denote an underlying similarity, a characteristic way of life that has grown out of identifiable historical events.

Generally the story of these events has not been told in terms of the West Indies or of the Caribbean but from the point of view of someone else; of the expansion of Europe, the struggle for empire, naval strategy, United States foreign policy, Canadian West Indian trade, Europe's trade in slaves and sugar. From the West Indian point of view there is a larger theme for which the Caribbean was the setting. It is that of the slow growth of a community of diverse racial origins out of a cruel and bloody beginning. This is something not easily seen from the outside. It was taking place in the West Indies in the very period when Froude was describing with accuracy the results of two centuries of English colonization: 'They were valued only for the wealth which they yielded, and society there has never achieved any

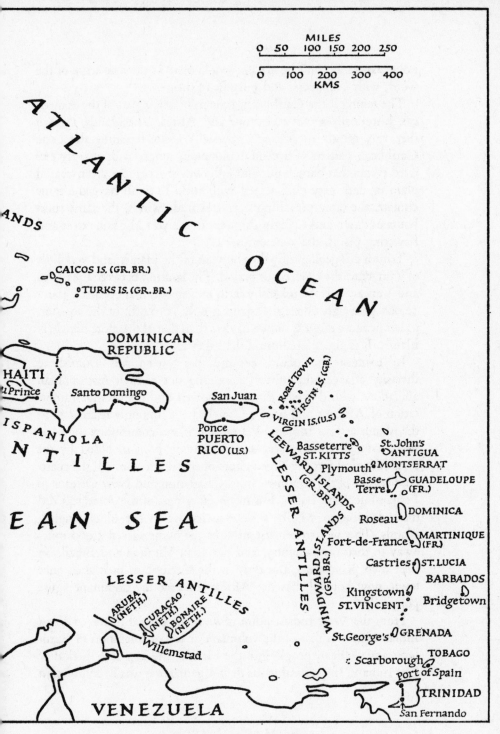

Political map of the Caribbean

noble aspect. . . . There are no people there in the true sense of the word, with a character and purpose of their own.'[2]

The setting is the Caribbean, geographically a part of the Americas, historically a part of Europe and Africa. The islands, though they vary greatly in size, are physically alike, repeating the basic Caribbean pattern of a central mountain range, with sharply serrated ridges that branch out and fall away sharply to a green coastal plain or dark grey cliffs edged with surf. They all have the same climate, the same prevailing northeast trade winds, the same short hours of dawn and twilight throughout the year, the same trees and flowering plants, the same crops.

Trinidad is geologically the youngest of the islands, and very little of it pre-dates the Cretaceous period. The last link between the island and Venezuela was broken by earth movements that occurred about 10,000 years ago. Since the island is only 10° north of the equator, its temperature range is somewhat less than that of the more northerly islands. It is also more humid than they are.

In contrast the island communities present an astonishing diversity of race and culture, springing out of their metropolitan affiliations with different European powers and the massive importation of Africans and people from India, commonly referred to in the islands as East Indians. Yet in each island community the basic social configuration is very similar, having been moulded by the same historical forces.[3] These forces operated also through the coastland region of the continent from Charleston and New Orleans to Pernambuco and Bahia, but in no other part of the Americas did there develop so wholly a slave-society as in the older English islands. This was so because most of the owners lived 5,000 miles away in their own country, and not as in Virginia and Brazil, on their own plantations. But only in the Caribbean, in islands once tragic now hopeful, has the African become the dominant figure politically.[4]

From the West Indian point of view the central theme in West Indian history is that of the voluntary or forced migration of European and African people into the islands, and at a later period of East Indians. In political terms their organization was in colonies; in social terms, in a caste system resting on slavery, each caste carrying its badge of race and colour; in economic terms, in imperial closed, circuit trading systems. The story develops through almost two centuries of fear, hatred, and a long agony of intolerance and injustice to the emancipation of the slaves; it continues through another century in which old cleavages narrowed and caste became class; and finally, in the last quarter of a century, it unfolds in the emergence of self-respecting independent nations, but with these still beset by insecurity, balancing on the razor-edge between success and disaster, striving desperately to reduce within themselves the areas of poverty and frustration.

There are two maps to look at. The first shows the setting of the islands in space, the second in time.

There are 51 inhabited islands in the Caribbean archipelago, ranging in size from Cuba with 44,164 square miles to Bequia which lies next to St Vincent, with an area of 7 square miles and a population of 2,600. The total land area of the inhabited islands is 87,291 square miles, larger than England, Scotland and Wales in Britain, or about the size of Pennsylvania and Virginia in the United States. The total population is of the order of 20 million. The former British West Indies have about one-eleventh of the land area, with 8,000 square miles, and one-sixth the population. Within themselves they exhibit the extraordinary disproportion in size which constitutes one of the chief problems of the region. Five of the large islands, Cuba, Hispaniola, Jamaica, Puerto Rico and Trinidad have 83,513 square miles of the total area. If all the islands, or most of them, formed one political unit this would not be so serious a matter; but as it is Cuba, and the Dominican Republic are Spanish-speaking republics, Haiti is a French-speaking republic, Jamaica and Trinidad are independent English-speaking countries, and Puerto Rico is a Spanish-speaking Commonwealth of the United States, and the flags of Britain, France, Holland and the United States fly over the other 46 islands.

Within themselves the West Indies exhibit the same disproportion, the islands of Jamaica and Trinidad having seven out of every eight acres of land, and four out of every five people. Eight islands share one-eighth of the land and one-fifth of the population. This extreme imbalance of resources and power between its units contributed to the collapse of the Federation of the West Indies. The importance of size as a factor in political and social development has been overlooked in the West Indies. In the contemporary world it often happens that small groups with limited resources lack trained men, and they develop and retain a limited conservative outlook. In the Caribbean, 'jealousies, rivalries, fears, and above all mutual ignorance tend to make each small island a museum in which archaic distinctions are carefully preserved.'[5]

The English, French and Dutch colonies in the archipelago were established a century and a quarter after the Spanish colonies. The difference in metropolitan associations makes Martinique more remote from neighbouring Barbados than is distant London; and Curacao, an hour's flight to the south from Barbados, is a foreign country as compared with Canada. Yet all these colonies have the same creole culture, the term 'creole' being used to mean what is native to the Caribbean. They all have the same historical base in colonialism, slavery and the plantation. As M. G. Smith points out:

> 'European and African elements predominate in fairly standard combinations and relationships. The ideal forms of institutional life, such as government, religion, family and kinship, law, property, education, economy and language are of European derivation: in consequence differing metropolitan associations produce differing versions of creole culture. . . .'[6]

For Africa contributed also, and the combination of African and European traditions is perhaps the most important feature of creole life. The intermingling extended to the physical, producing the brown people of the West Indies, offspring of European and African.

> 'This negro-white complex which has been formative for the West Indies diverges sharply in its racial and cultural components. In this area Negroes outnumber whites markedly, and

have done so for centuries; but European institutions and cultural models predominate. . . . The West Indian-bred white is not culturally European nor is the West Indian-bred black culturally African.'[7]

The combination of European institutions and language with African predominance in numbers makes the West Indies different from any other new-world society. The mould was shaped in the 1650s and lasted until all African slaves in British colonies were set free by an Act of Emancipation in 1834. For long the African connection was ignored or regarded with disfavour, but today Africa is a powerful symbol in the West Indies as we shall see when we examine West Indian literature and folk beliefs. The Haitian poet Roumain was prophetic of the West Indian mood of the present day in his lines 'I have kept your memory, Africa. You are in me.'[8]

The English settlements in New England and in the Caribbean belong to the same period. The Mayflower Compact was drawn up in 1620, three years before Thomas Warner founded the first English settlement in the Caribbean at St Kitts. Winthrop and his settlers arrived at Salem four years after John Powell and his party of tobacco planters set up their homes at Hole Town in Barbados. Between 1630 and 1642 the great migration from England to the Massachusetts Bay colony was under way, 16,000 people emigrating to Massachusetts in the years when other parties of Englishmen were settling in Antigua, Montserrat and Nevis. Connecticut and Maine were being settled in the decade when Jamaica was taken from the Spaniards in 1655.

The West Indies were some of England's oldest colonies, and they proved to be among her last, the colonial relationship surviving for more than three centuries. The length of the relationship is significant. It lasted in Jamaica and Trinidad and Tobago until 1962 when both these countries became independent. It still exists in many of the islands. Colonialism, however important, was an incident in the history of Nigeria and Ghana, Kenya or Uganda; but it is the whole history of the West Indies, and as a West Indian novelist has pointed out, it has a deeper meaning for the West Indian than for the African who 'has never been wholly severed from the cradle of continuous culture and tradition. . . . Colonialism is the very base and structure of the West Indian's cultural awareness.'[9]

The third element, along with African slavery, the system of East Indian indentured labour and the long colonial relationship, is the plantation; a rigid economic organization for the mass production of one crop, conceived of as a socio-economic unity with its own paternal set of relationships between master and worker.[10] The economic base fell out of the system in the middle of the nineteenth century. In some parts of the West Indies the sugar plantation on the old system almost disappeared. In other parts it lasted because it was able to exploit cheap labour, the 'located' African labourer in Barbados, the East Indian indentured labourer in Trinidad. The sugar industry has been reorganized and new relationships established between those who manage and those who labour, so that the West Indies has adjusted itself to twentieth-century industrial concepts and methods. But for the greater part of West Indian history the plantation system reinforced the colour-scale values and the social organization of the slave-colony.

The West Indian story is not that of empire, though the islands were prizes of empire in the eighteenth century. The breathtaking natural beauty of the islands, about which Columbus wrote with enthusiasm in his famous first letter to the Spanish Sovereigns, is not the chief matter; nor the romantic and often savage history that involved great men like Raleigh, 'who like a star fell when the firmament was shaked', nor ruthless leaders like Henry Morgan nor debased perverts like L'Ollonais; nor even the record of wretched soldiers dying like flies of the bloody flux, yellow jack and black vomit before Cartagena or on the Morne in St Lucia or in the fields of Haiti. Rather, it is essentially the story of white, brown and black men and how the relationship between them of master and slave changed and gave way to that of equality; of freedom coming with agonizing slowness; of those who died for it; and of the establishment of communities in which the key words are not tolerance, which implies that something must be tolerated, nor acceptance, but rather natural human feeling, affection, respect.

2   Meeting Place of Two Worlds

THE CARIBBEAN was the first permanent point of contact between people living on the east and west coasts of the Atlantic Ocean. In Hispaniola, Cuba, Jamaica and Puerto Rico, the four large islands that form the northern half of the archipelago, the first meeting in history took place between the brown man of old America, the white man from Europe and the black man from Africa; for whether singly or by the shipload, as servant or as slave, the black man entered the Americas alongside the European.

Contact was first established by Christopher Columbus when, on 12 October 1492, 32 days out from the Azores, he sighted Guanahani, an island in the Bahamas group. He had set out from Spain to find a westward route to Cathay. It was common knowledge among the geographers of his time that the world was round, but it was assumed that only the Atlantic lay between Western Europe and the lands of the east. Using such information as was available to him Columbus calculated that he had to make a transAtlantic journey of 2,400 nautical miles to reach Cathay. He had already exceeded that distance when he made his landfall in Guanahani. Being certain that he had reached the East he gave the name of Indians to the brownskinned sturdy people who met him, and he called their lands the Indies. Having established a small settlement in Hispaniola he hurried back to Spain with the joyful news of the discovery of a safe westerly searoute to the east. In the four voyages that he made between 1492 and 1504 he explored the line of islands in the archipelago from Trinidad and Tobago northwards, and part of the coast of Honduras, searching always for the spices and gold of Cathay. His belief that he had found the Indies comforted him

15

during the bitter years of rejection that ended with his death in a small house in Valladolid in May 1506. He was many thousands of miles out in his reckoning. Without knowing it, he revealed another world to Europe. The continent he found bears not his name but, in the view of many historians, that of another Italian, Amerigo Vespucci. Later the islands to which he came were called the West Indies to distinguish them from the true Indies. The people he called Indians are now termed Amerindians. Columbus was the first traveller from modern Europe to reach America without knowing that he had arrived.

With care and passion Spain entered upon the task of settling the new lands that she claimed by right of prior discovery. The meeting between the indigenous people of the islands and the newcomers from Europe turned out to be a collision between two civilizations widely separated in time. The native Arawak people, the first dis-coverers of the islands, had migrated from the region of the Orinoco and the Guianas, bridging with their canoes the gulf between each island. The European bridged the wide gulf of the Atlantic, but no way was found of bridging the gulf between Arawak and European, the stone age and the Renaissance. The Arawaks, and in the course of time the Caribs of the eastern islands, were wiped out in the col-lision between dug-out canoes and ships, bows and arrows and cannon, sharply pointed reeds and swords, naked men on foot and horsemen in armour. The extermination proceeded all the more rapidly because the Arawaks had no natural immunity to smallpox and measles.

In Cuba, an Arawak chief, Hatuey, who led a resistance move-ment against the Spaniards, pointed to the main reason for the destruction of his people. He uncovered a basket filled with gold, and said, 'Here is their lord, whom they serve and adore . . . for him they persecute us, for him they have killed our parents, all our people and our neighbours.'[11] The Spaniards enslaved the Arawaks and when the supply ran short, slave-raiding expeditions were sent out, some south to Trinidad, others into the Bahamas, the raids being so costly in human life that one Spaniard declared a ship without com-pass, map or guide, only following the track of the dead bodies, could find its way from the Bahamas to Hispaniola. The Caribbean had its Middle Passage before the Atlantic.[12]

The destruction of the native people was more complete in the Caribbean than anywhere else in America. The islands were comparatively small. There was nowhere for the Arawaks and Caribs to go. But the Arawak lived on as part of that American world of fact and fable which disturbed the European imagination and took it captive. The Indies was a part of that world in which it proved so difficult to distinguish between fact and fancy, the reality of Aztec and Inca splendour and the dream of El Dorado, the scourge of syphilis and the legend of the Amazons, the Pacific shining like a silver shield before the eyes of Balboa and the Fountain of Perpetual Youth that ageing Ponce de Leon never found. Also, moral questions, nagging as toothache, arose out of the encounter in the islands between primitive and modern, Arcadian simplicity and Renaissance subtlety, Caliban and Prospero.

The result was a sharp break in the history of the islands. In the temperate regions of the continent, in Canada and the United States, Chile and Argentina, the European slowly became complete master. The sense of historic continuity is with Western Europe. In the region that extends from the Rio Grande south through Colombia and Brazil to the River Plate the Indian survived in large numbers, and there sprang up a mestizo culture with roots in civilizations that pre-date Columbus. But the Indians of the islands perished. The newcomers took over elements of the old culture with the use of food crops like cassava, maize and sweet potato, the smoking of tobacco, the making of fish-pots and pirogues or dugouts, the use of place-names like Haiti, land of mountains, and Jamaica, land of wood and water, but the history of the West Indies that we know begins abruptly with a clearly marked event, the arrival of Columbus. Unlike tropical Africa and the eastern tropics the Caribbean islands have neither indigenous people nor ancient cultures and civilizations.

The Caribbean became a part of the frontier of Western Europe. The heady new imperialism that produced New Granada and New Spain, New France, New England, New Amsterdam and Nova Scotia won its first foothold in the Caribbean, in Hispaniola, Little

Spain. It began with the arrival of 17 ships and 1,200 men off the north coast of the island in November 1494. The fleet was under the command of Columbus. The year before, after announcing to the Spanish sovereigns his success in finding a way to the Indies, he had urged on them a policy of settlement with a first instalment of 2,000 settlers, the founding of three or four towns, the building of churches and the employment of priests for the conversion of the Indians. The settlers were to search for gold. For their encouragement, Ferdinand and Isabella decreed that any settler might keep one-third of the gold he found, 'and the remaining two-thirds will be for Us'.[13]

Aboard the ships there were cattle, swine, sheep, goats, horses, as well as seeds and plants. Some of the livestock died during the voyage. The survivors were put ashore and multiplied prodigiously. The process was simple. A letter written to the Emperor Charles V, from Santo Domingo, 24 years after the introduction of these animals, reported that herds of cows numbering 30 or 40, having been branded, wandered off and three or four years later were found in the hills to the number of three or four hundred.[14] These herds of wild pigs and wild cattle must have assisted in exterminating the Arawaks by devouring their patches of maize and trampling their fields of cassava.

There was less success with cereals. Wheat and barley failed. Rice did moderately well. Bananas, lemons, and oranges flourished in spite of strange pests against which the colonists could do little; like the plague of ants that devoured the citrus and pomegranate trees around San Juan del Puerto Rico, leaving them black and withered as if they had been struck by lightning.[15]

The fleet of ships that moved slowly to an anchorage off the north coast of Hispaniola that November, within easy reach of vivid green fields and unbroken forests, was Spain transporting into the Carib-bean her way of life, her language, creed, and her political insti-tutions. The ships were Europe, introducing into America her skills and arts, replacing the limited techniques of the stone-age islanders with the technology of the Renaissance; and for the first time turning her face away from that old inland sea that for so long had been the centre of her world.

Aboard one of the ships in the fleet of 1494 were some half-dry cuttings of sugar-cane, collected from the Canary Islands. The withered brown shoots responded at once to the new environment, growing so that it was wonderful to see, the cane as thick as a man's wrist and as tall as the height of two men of medium stature. So Alfonso de Zuazo declared, writing from Santo Domingo.[16]

A few settlers planted patches of sugar-cane. The island had all that was needed for sugar production: a fertile soil, an abundant supply of water, wood for fuel. Mills were built and workmen brought from the Canary Islands who were expert in making sugar; for, unlike oranges and bananas, sugar is not a crop but a product, one that must be made within two days of the cutting of the sugar-cane lest fermentation begin in the stalks, rendering them useless.

One thing more was needed. Labour had to be found to till the fields, grow and harvest the sugar-cane; and there was need, declared a Spanish historian, for 'at least eighty or one-hundred Negroes working all the time and even one hundred and twenty or more'.[17]

Spain took the sugar industry seriously. It was treated as a pioneer industry, incentives being provided through easy loans from the government, grants of land on favourable terms, and other valuable concessions.[18] These were of special importance to sugar-producers in Cuba in the nineteenth century,[19] but at this early period investors put their money into the expeditions on the mainland, for every man wanted 'to ascend in rank or win great wealth'.[20] Mexico and Peru drew colonists and investors away from the islands. What conquistador would plough a few arrobas of land in an island when on the mainland El Dorado, 'the golden man' might be a reality?

A society sprang up based largely on a pastoral economy, very unlike that of the eighteenth-century slave-and-sugar plantations of the Eastern Caribbean and Jamaica. There was a smaller proportion of Africans to Europeans, more intermarriage of white and mulatto, a larger number of free people of colour.

The Spaniard introduced the sugar-cane into the Caribbean, and he also introduced the African. A window on the future opened in 1518, when a ship arrived at Santo Domingo with a cargo of African slaves. There were already Africans in the new world. One was with Balboa at the discovery of the Pacific, another with Cortez in Mexico, another with Pizarro on his first visit to Peru. When Ovando was Governor, Africans were in Hispaniola as slaves. But up to this time the organized slave trade was in Arawak Indians, not in Africans.

Las Casas urged that the only way of saving the Arawak was to enslave the African. In Spain he pleaded with the Emperor, begging him to grant a licence for importing Africans, twelve for each settler. He had seen African slaves at work in Hispaniola and had noted that they were tougher and more resilient than the Indians. Courtiers added their persuasions to that of the priest, and in 1518 Charles V granted to one of his favourite courtiers a licence to supply 4,000 Negro slaves to Hispaniola.

In later years Las Casas suffered anguish of spirit at what he had done and condemned all slavery, Arawak or African. It was too late. The first black cargo had arrived. An organized trade in African slaves had begun. The ship swinging at anchor at Santo Domingo, within sight of the Cathedral in the centre of the city, was the first in an innumerable fleet of slave ships that traversed the Atlantic year after year for more than $3\frac{1}{2}$ centuries. The 4,000 Africans for whom Charles V granted a licence were the first victims in a forced movement of some 15 million people from Africa into the Americas.

All, save the man most closely concerned, agreed that Africa was the one and only hope. Dominican Fathers in Hispaniola urged that the labour of one African was worth more than that of four Arawaks.[21] Settlers emphasized that the development of the island depended on Negroes.[22] The chief urgency was for Negroes.[23] From Cuba colonists petitioned for Negroes, two or three hundred at least, and free of duty. The Bishop of San Juan pointed out that only the importation of hundreds of Africans could restore prosperity to the island.[24] In this way it came about that the Europeanization of the new world involved also the Africanization of the Caribbean and of the coastland of America from the Carolinas to Brazil.

At first only Spain was concerned, but in 1527 an English ship appeared off Santo Domingo, making a reconnaissance of the Spanish

Indies. French and English seamen had already begun to attack Spanish shipping but this arrival of 1527 is the first recorded entry of a foreign ship into the Caribbean. After taking some supplies by force further west along the coast it set out to sea, and was not heard from again.

The meaning was clear. Other ships followed. Smugglers, defying Spain, sought cargoes of tobacco, hides and cochineal along the coasts of the Caribbean. Traders like John Hawkins entered the closed sea, seeking to persuade Spanish colonists by tongue and gun to buy cargoes of African slaves. Drake spread terror and destruction through the Spanish Main, and his Queen, Elizabeth I, emphasized that the sea and air were common to all men.[25] The unknown ship of 1527 heralded the establishment of colonies in the islands by other European powers and the incorporation of each of these colonies into the exclusive trading system of each metropolitan power.

3 An Island is a World

LATE IN THE SIXTEENTH CENTURY the rivals of Spain made their first attempts at establishing permanent settlements in Spanish America. They began, not in the islands but along the 'wild coast', concerning which Dutch and English traders brought back favour-able reports, a fever-stricken stretch of low-lying land between the mouth of the Orinoco and Portuguese settlements in Brazil, out of easy reach of Spanish forces based on Caracas. In 1498, when he discovered Trinidad, Columbus had become aware of the vast rivers of Venezuela, which flowed out of Paradise itself. He had written 'I do not think there is known in the world a river so big and so deep'. In 1595 Raleigh sailed these waters, the gateway to 'golden Manoa', where 'Orinoco in his pride rolled to the main a rival sea of roaring war', and Guiana offered its red gold, 'a country that hath yet her maidenhead, never sacked, burnt nor wrought'.

South of the Orinoco, along the wild coast where primitive War-rau Indians lived in huts and grew manioc in clearings in the humid heat of the forests, Dutch and English settlers struggled to make settlements and plant tobacco. Heat and fever defeated most attempts. The Dutch succeeded in founding colonies along the Essequibo in 1616 and the Berbice in 1624, but the English attempts came to nothing; yet indirectly these failures led to the settlement of some of the islands in the Caribbean. At the time Spain held Cuba, His-paniola, Jamaica, Puerto Rico and Trinidad. The Caribs occupied most of the other islands. They beat off the first attempts of the English to settle, wiping out a band that landed in St Lucia in 1605, and another in Grenada in 1609. The first success came when Thomas Warner, on his way back from Guiana, landed at St

Christopher in 1622. Being attracted by the beauty of the little island and the apparent fertility of the soil, and encouraged by the fact that he was able to make friends with the Carib king, he determined to found a colony there. He obtained the necessary capital and patronage in England and in 1623 established in St Christopher the first permanent English settlement in the Caribbean. A second colony was founded in 1624 when John Powell, on his way back to England from Brazil, landed at Barbados and claimed the island for England. Other islands were soon settled by English colonists; Nevis in 1628, Antigua and Montserrat in 1632. Twenty years later, in 1655, an expedition sent out by Cromwell captured Jamaica from Spain.

The French and Dutch were slower off the mark. Soon after Warner settled in St Kitts a French privateer, d'Esnambuc, landed with a small party of Frenchmen, and Warner sensibly agreed to share the island with him, for the Caribs were becoming restive and allies were welcome. Not until 1635 however, did Richelieu organize the *Compagnie des Isles d'Amerique*. In that year the French settled in Martinique and Guadeloupe.

The main effort of the Dutch to gain empire was made against the Portuguese in Brazil. In the Caribbean they contented themselves with acquiring small islands that were chiefly of value as bases for smuggling and trade. Between 1630 and 1640 they occupied Curacao, Saba, St Martin and St Eustatius and Tobago.

Through the establishment of these various colonies the archipelago reflected the chief cultural and political differences of Europe. At the same time the expansion of sugar plantations led to a vast increase in the importation of Africans. This will be discussed in greater detail in the following chapter, but one result was to increase greatly the diversity of race and culture in the Caribbean. White and black Dutchmen administer the affairs of Aruba, black Frenchmen from Martinique elect deputies to their Assembly in Paris, black Englishmen rule Barbados, East Indian and African Trinidadians share citizenship with French and Spanish creoles, English, Syrians, Jews, Lebanese and Portuguese; blond blueeyed people, many of them Englishspeaking, live in a capital town named after Gustavus of Sweden as citizens of the French island of St Barthelemy. Not far to the west, in Puerto Rico, swarthy people of mixed descent, citizens of the United States, cherish their Spanish cultural heritage.

The buildings repeat the contrasts and variations, revealing the innumerable ways in which West Indian history became a footnote to the history of Western Europe. In Willemstad, capital of Curacao, steep-gabled Dutch houses painted in gay colours look across a narrow channel called St Anna Bay to a floating market of schooners and sloops, where Venezuelans sell cargoes of oranges, green-skinned papaya, green and yellow bananas, charcoal and flustered hens. To the north, in Bridgetown, the capital of Barbados, Nelson stands in a miniature Trafalgar Square, his monument made to scale, and in neighbouring Martinique the statue of Josephine overlooks the Savane and French shops and cafés beyond. In St Georges in Grenada, Georgian houses of red brick, roofed with handsome fish-tiles from Martinique,[26] look out on a bay of indigo blue that dances with glittering points of reflected light. Each island is a world insulated from its neighbours by the sea and isolated by long-established colonial frontiers.

Even within one group of colonies there were important differences, for history took a different course with some than with others.[27] The English-speaking islands, the former British West Indies provide possibly the best examples of this. Up to the time when Trinidad was taken from Spain in 1798, it was a Spanish colony inhabited by Spanish and French settlers who had a number of slaves. It was never a slave economy on the scale of Jamaica. Though it had a number of plantations worked by slave labour its sugar estates were developed not so much by African, as by East Indian labourers. Grenada, St Lucia and Dominica did not become slave-and-sugar plantations in the way that Barbados, Antigua and St Kitts did, because of their rugged terrain. In the wars against France in the eighteenth century, some islands changed hands more than once, each change disrupting and modifying the way of life in the island. St Lucia suffered most since it changed hands 13 times. The Windward Islands are predominantly Roman Catholic, and the people speak a French patois as well as English, whereas Barbados and the Leeward Islands, which have an almost unbroken connection with England from the time of their first settlement, are chiefly Protestant and wholly English-speaking. With them is Jamaica, which, after a feverish period of smuggling, piracy and buccaneering, turned to sugar, and by 1700 was taking the lead as a sugar producer.

Early records from Jamaica and Barbados show how English institutions were introduced into the islands in as natural a way as the Spaniards introduced their system of government through the municipality, and their religious and educational institutions. The method of running the affairs of a parish through a Vestry, developed in England by the Tudors, was transferred to the older English colonies in the Caribbean, the freeholders of the parish electing those who for 12 months would levy rates for poor relief, the upkeep of roads, payment of the clergymen and teachers, the control of vagabonds and so on.

In Jamaica, the Justices and Vestry of the Parish of St Elizabeth at a meeting in 1695, ordered that for levying rates 'Negroes young and old be valued at ten pounds a Head, and cattle of all sorts at Thirty Shillings a head and sheep and goats at five pounds a score and that the tax be levied at 12/6 for every hundred pounds. . . .'[28]

This is in contrast with Trinidad under Spanish rule. There, as in the other Spanish colonies and as in Spain itself, administration was highly centralized. Spanish governors in Trinidad had autocratic powers, but these were limited by the fact that sentences pronounced by them had to be confirmed by a royal 'audiencia' in Caracas, and by the special inquiry the 'residencia' held towards the close of a governor's term of office. In Port of Spain the municipal council, the Cabildo, also exercised a restraining influence on the central government.

Colonialism involved the transfer of the legal and governmental institutions of the metropolitan country. It also encouraged hostility and rivalry between the islands so that the traditional Caribbean outlook became one of isolationism rather than of co-operation. In an article published in 1952,[29] Dr Eric Williams who later became Prime Minister of Trinidad and Tobago, pointed out that distance and the absence of adequate communications fostered the isolationism which had resulted from the international rivalry that dominated

Caribbean history. He emphasized that even if these deeply in-
grained characteristics of Caribbean society were magically to
disappear, cheap and easy communications be established, four-and-
a-half centuries of foreign hegemony be blotted out and the area
transformed into one fraternity, the two fundamental obstacles to
unity would still remain, those of a common body of knowledge and
the language barrier.

Trade was so organized that it added to the rivalry and jealousy of
island for island. Spain had shown how to put into practice the
prevailing doctrine that a colony existed for the benefit of the mother-
country; that all its imports and exports should be with and through
the mother-country, and that a nation made itself secure and powerful through a carefully organized colonial trade from which other
nations were excluded. The classic pattern was that in which the
colony provided raw materials for the metropole, and bought from
her all its manufactured goods and even its food.

Spain carried this mercantile policy to extreme lengths, regulating
in detail its imperial trade to the point where all imports and exports
had to pass through one port, Cadiz, so as to make control easier.
Although neither France nor England went so far, there was no
difference in outlook and philosophy between them and Spain.[30]
France did not change her basic philosophy of mercantilism during
300 years of colonial rule in Martinique and Guadeloupe. England
retained the system in essence under Crown Colony rule. A trade
barrier was added to the political boundaries of nationality.

For a period during the eighteenth century the West Indian
islands were the prize colonies of Britain's empire, corresponding
closely to the ideal. Economists were ecstatic at the perfection of a
system in which the West Indies were 'producing what we want, and
wanting what we produce'.[31] They pointed to the fact that 'from the
crown of the head to the sole of the foot, a West India planter is
clothed by the manufacturers of Great Britain and Ireland. Five
hundred thousand Negroes are constantly clad by the clothiers of
Yorkshire and Wiltshire . . .'[32] Calculators and statisticians joined
in the hymn of praise, 'that the glory and grandeur of England has
been advanced more by sugar than any other commodity, wool not

excepted'.[33] The West India planters rubbed in the fact of their importance to England, by building up a powerful lobby in Parliament to preserve a society that rested on the shoulders of hundreds of thousands of African slaves and the cultivation of one crop. The West Indian landscape is full of reminders of that period of dizzy prosperity and power. Overlooking the south coast of St Kitts, an island of 68 square miles round which one can drive in two hours, stands Brimstone Hill, built in 1793 on a precipitous rocky hill at such an outlay of money and labour that it was called the Gibraltar of the West. The naval counterpart is in Antigua, at English Harbour, where the eighteenthcentury buildings at sealevel and the massive battlements on Shirley Heights once provided English fleets with an impregnable base. The Morne Fortuné above the harbour of Castries in St Lucia, where in 1796 John Moore kept guard with 4,000 men who were soon reduced to 1,000 by yellow fever, Fort St Louis and Fort Bourbon that protected Fort de France across the narrow channel in Martinique and strongly fortified Port Royal in Jamaica, a thousand miles away to the west, speak of the high place that small sugarislands then held in Britain's first empire.

Since all the islands produced sugar, trade intensified the rivalry even between those that were attached to the same metropole. Sugar planters in Barbados objected strongly to the cultivation of sugar in St Kitts.[34] The proposal for adding the French sugar island, Guadeloupe, to the English islands in the peace of 1763 was bitterly attacked by the West India interest, since more sugar would mean cheaper sugar and consequently smaller profits for them. Their pressure influenced England's decision to give up Guadeloupe and keep Canada, to the delight of the French who thought they had got much the better of the bargain.

Competition and isolationism rooted in 300 years of colonial rule produced builtin attitudes of distrust. These attitudes contributed to the downfall of the fouryearold Federation of the West Indies in 1962.

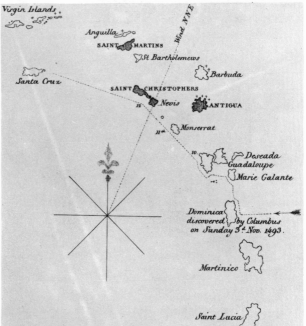

1 In 1492 the Italian explorer Christopher Columbus first reached the Indies. He established a settlement in Hispaniola, seen in this sixteenth-century engraving.

2 Columbus took this route through the Eastern Caribbean in 1493.

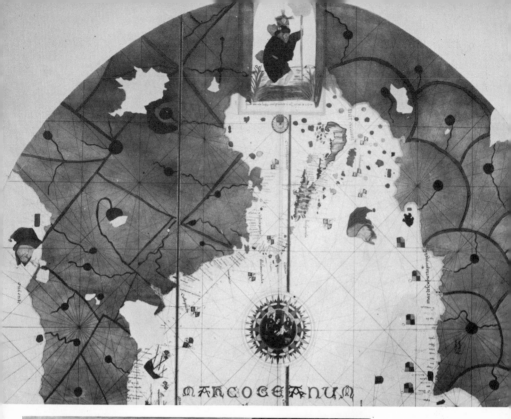

MARCOCEANUM

3 The first map of the world to include the islands of the Caribbean was made by Juan de la Cosa in 1500.

4 The Spanish tried to shut out other European powers from the Caribbean. An oil painting by Eugenio Caxes of a Spanish attack on St Kitts.

5 The Spanish priest, Bartolomé de las Casas, advocated the importation of slaves from Africa in order to preserve the native Arawaks of the islands.

6 Many of the native Arawak people were tortured or burnt by the Spanish in Hispaniola.

7 During the mid-seventeenth century buccaneers and pirates ravaged the Spanish Main. A Spanish Armada was destroyed by Captain Henry Morgan.

8 Henry Morgan (1635–88), a ruthless buccaneer known as the 'Uncrowned King of Port Royal', became Lieutenant-Governor of Jamaica.

9, 10 Pirates such as Blackbeard (*above*), and women pirates like Ann Bonney and Mary Read (*below*) spread terror through the Caribbean.

11 France also sought control of the islands. She settled in Guadeloupe in 1635.

12 Barbados was founded as a British Colony in 1625. This map dates from 1657.

Haiti gained its independence in 1804 through the victories of Toussaint, Dessalines and Christophe over the French. This is Christophe, who had himself crowned Emperor of Haiti.

The sugar industry has had a profound influence on the history of the islands. A Sugar Boiling House the early nineteenth century.

15 Relics of European imperial rivalry at Spanish Town, Jamaica. The Rodney Memorial commemorates the British victory of Admiral Rodney over the French in 1782.

16 (*left*) This is at Fort-de-France, Martinique, which has been a French colony since 1635.

17 (*below*) The Dutch also established strongholds in the West Indies. This is at Aruba where many of the buildings are Dutch in character.

4   Africa in Force

IN TERMS OF NUMBERS, Africa took possession of the West Indies in the eighteenth century. During that period the expansion in the English colonies of sugar-production by means of African labour resulted in the population structure of present-day Barbados and Jamaica.[35] In Barbados 95 out of every 100 people are black or coloured and 5 are white. In Antigua and St Kitts 2 out of every 100 are white. The proportion is lower still in Dominica and Jamaica where 1 out of every 100 persons is white. Numerically, other racial groups are unimportant. The two chief elements only in the population are the brown and the black, and the black is predominant. In Jamaica just over 17 per cent of the population are coloured, 78 per cent are black; in Antigua 12 per cent are coloured, 85 per cent black; in St Kitts 86 per cent are black. In Montserrat, 92 per cent of the population are black and 6 per cent coloured. The population in these islands has the usual Caribbean characteristics of a wide range of pigmentation based on the intermingling of black and white, but predominantly it is African.[36]

The contrast with the early years of English colonization is striking. In Barbados in 1645 there were 18,000 white persons able to bear arms. By 1667 that number had dropped to 8,300. Over the same period the number of African slaves increased from 5,680 to 82,023.[37] In the Leeward Islands the trend was the same. In 1678 Montserrat had 2,683 white people and 993 Negroes; in 1727 there were 1,143 white people and 5,855 Negroes.[38] The total numbers were much larger in Jamaica, where in 1670 there were 8,000 white persons and 9,504 slaves. In 1787 there were 25,000 whites and 210,894 slaves.[39]

With the exception of Haiti, the population structure is very different in all the other islands. This is so because the development of the sugar plantation took place in Trinidad, Cuba and Puerto Rico in the nineteenth century. The English slave trade was abolished in 1807. The trans-Atlantic trade in African slaves was virtually ended in 1865. The Puerto Rican plantations were worked by slaves and also by free coloured peasants left landless by the spread of the estates.[40] In Trinidad where the sugar estates owed their development to the East Indian indentured labourer, there are two large racial groupings, Negro and East Indian. Out of every 100 people 46 are Negro, 14 mixed or coloured, and 35 East Indian.[41]

In the first quarter-century of English settlement in Barbados and the Leeward Islands the white man was in the majority.[42] The chief crop was tobacco and the chief agricultural unit the small holding. The field workers were mostly European. They were there to grow tobacco, indigo and cotton for sale in Europe, so as to produce dividends for investors who had put up the money to equip them with tools and seed and ship them abroad.

In the first years of settlement, many of the migrants were people who sold themselves into slavery for three or five years in return for their passage, clothing and food, and at the end of the period, 300 pounds of tobacco or the like. They migrated mostly from the southwest counties of England, and from Suffolk, Essex and Hertfordshire.[43] They moved of their own will, leaving behind them the chronic unemployment that plagued England. Other emigrants went from the northwest of France, especially from Normandy and Brittany, to the French islands of Martinique and Guadeloupe, poor people for the most part who had grown up in the seigneurial tradition and knew what serfdom meant.[44] Thomas Warner, founder of the first English settlement, was a Suffolk man, and Pierre d'Esnambuc, pioneer of French colonization in the Caribbean, was a Norman. The flow of voluntary migrants lasted for some years though the voyage was long and the loss of life at sea often heavy. Warner, on his outward voyage in 1636, had 'great sickness and mortality; not twenty out of two hundred escaped, about forty having died'.[45] Out of a party of 520 that d'Esnambuc recruited from Normandy and Brittany, people 'not accustomed to the fatigues of the sea', 250 died.[46]

The new colonies were valued because they produced a tropical crop that yielded good profits and were a vent for the unemployed of the mother-country, for artisans and tradesmen who were out of work, evicted tenants and sober-minded people seeking to better themselves. Looking forward from the 1580s the preacher Richard Hakluyt had prophesied that the time was approaching when the English would 'share and part stakes . . . both with the Spaniard and the Portugal in part of America . . .'.[47] By 1650 the time had come. Every traveller returned from across the Atlantic with tales of wealth and of wonder. Adventurous men seeking for betterment looked to America and the Indies even though dramatists like Chapman laughed at Captain Seagull's picture of Virginia where 'gold is more plentiful than copper is with us. . . . Why man, all their dripping pans and chamber pots are pure gold. . . . You may be an alderman there and never be a scavenger. You may be a nobleman and never a slave. . . .'[48]

A period of slavery awaited the indentured servants, who, being bound to a master for a limited period, were exploited mercilessly. When the supply of voluntary migrants began to fall off a trade sprang up in convicts and prisoners of war, adults spirited away and kidnapped children. The islands could take not only the poor and unemployed but also the social outcasts. A century earlier Ferdinand and Isabella of Spain had ordered that murderers, counterfeiters, sodomists and thieves should go and serve in Hispaniola under the command of Christopher Columbus. Other European nations also took the view that colonies were a valuable dumping ground for malefactors. Richard Hakluyt put the argument eloquently:

'Yea, if we would behold with the eye of pity how all our prisons are pestered and filled up with able men to serve their country which for small robberies are daily hanged up in great numbers, some twenty at a clap out of one jail (as was seen at the last assize at Rochester) we would hasten . . . the deducting of some colonies of our superfluous people into those temperate and fertile parts of America . . .'[49]

Some bondservants did well. A St Kitts planter, Christopher Jeaffreson, writing in 1680, said that out of the humours that first peopled the islands and made them a kind of Bedlam for a short time, had come many solid and sober men.[50] But Henry Whistler, in his *Journal of the West Indian Expedition*, 1654-5, found Barbados 'the dunghill whereon England doth cast forth its rubbish . . . a rogue in England will hardly make a cheater here; a bawd brought over puts on a demure comportment, a whore if handsome makes the wife for some rich planter . . .'.[51] And one of the leaders of the expedition, General Venables, said that the poor whites he recruited in Barbados and the Leeward Islands were the most profane and debauched people he had ever seen.[52]

The quality of white indentured servants declined, and the number of voluntary immigrants dwindled at the same time that sugar-cane began to displace tobacco and the demand for labour began to increase. Stirred to protest by the shortage, little Montserrat reminded the Lords of Plantations and Trades in London that no colony could be developed without a supply of white servants and Negroes. A flourishing trade in white servants sprang up and Jeaffreson, seeing a chance of making a profit for himself and his partners out of the purchase of English convicts, urged that the islands would welcome even the spawn spewed out by Bridewell and Newgate since there was no jailbird so incorrigible that he could not be reformed. In 1686 Jeaffreson himself, assisted by a few friends, escorted a ragged band of 38 malefactors from Newgate to a ship waiting in the Thames, being anxious to get his precious cargo aboard safely.[53]

The demand for servants and slaves increased sharply with the introduction of sugar-cane cultivation and of sugar technology. With extraordinary speed, sugar took hold of the islands, after one or two early failures. Trezel, a Dutch merchant of Rouen, attempted to establish sugar-cane cultivation in Martinique in 1639, and later, in the 1640s, the Governor of the island, Charles Houel, introduced the proper processes of cultivation and manufacture. By 1650 some Barbados planters were producing sugar of fair quality on their estates. Eight years later de Poincy, Governor of the French part of

St Kitts, established a sugar plantation there with three sugar mills, and there was also a plantation with some mills at Cayonne on the island's north coast.

A revolution followed. Sugar-cane, as the first planters in Hispaniola knew, is a rich man's crop. To be profitable, it has to be grown in large units. Its introduction into Barbados radically changed the economy of the island, which up to then was based on small holdings worked by white owners and their white and black slaves. There were more than 11,000 of these smallholdings in 1645, but by 1665 they had been displaced by 745 plantations. The white tenants and smallholders migrated to neighbouring islands or to Jamaica, or went off to join the buccaneers and pirates that were plaguing the region.

Other crops were displaced, for sugar was profitable and claimed all the suitable land. Indigo and cotton fell far behind. The economy of the sugar islands was based on the large-scale cultivation of one crop. Dependence on one crop was complete, and so was dependence on one market, for the sugar island was knitted closely into the trading system of the mother-country. The topography of Barbados and St Kitts made it possible for practically all their cultivable land to be put under sugar-cane. They remain sugar islands more completely than any other West Indian territory. In Barbados 56 out of every 100 acres are fit for cultivation and seven out of every eight of the cultivable acres are under sugar-cane.[54] More than 90 per cent of the domestic exports of the island consist of sugar, molasses and sugar confectionery. In St Kitts one-third of the total area is under sugar-cane and sugar and molasses bring in 90 per cent of the island's earnings.

In the process, the African labourer displaced the white bond-servant. In Nevis the total white population declined from 3,521 in 1678 to 1,118 in 1756 and over the same period the Negro population rose from 3,860 to 8,380.[55] These changes were part of the general trend to which reference has been made. They followed directly on the change-over from tobacco planting to the double process of cultivating sugar-cane and the manufacture of sugar, and these were linked with the importation of Africans.

The portion of Africa that was involved extended from the Senegal River to the mouth of the Congo and beyond to Angola and Benguela; in distance approximately the length of the coastline of Europe from Trondheim to Gibraltar. Many diverse African nations and kingdoms occupied this vast stretch of country, including the brown-skinned, long-haired Fulani, the brown Wolofs and Mandingos who are both Muslim people, the proud and warlike Ashanti, Ewe-speaking tribes, Fanti, Yorubas, Dahomians, Ibos and Ibibios, Efiks, and people of the Bantu group from the Congo and Angola.

Two million Africans were imported from this region into the English colonies in the Caribbean between 1680 and 1786, a significant part of the 15 million taken to the Americas between 1518 and the year in which the trade was suppressed, 1865. The cargoes of black men and women, oiled and made ready for sale on slave ships at anchor at Bridgetown, Basseterre, St Johns or Kingston and the slaves put up for auction in slave markets in the capital town of each island, were a very small fraction of the millions of black and white people who through 400 years were caught up in this trade that changed the history of three continents and caused the destruction of many millions of human beings. The trade linked the African slaves on West Indian plantations with 'hands' in new factories in Manchester and Birmingham that turned out goods for the West African trade, with merchants and seamen in Liverpool, Bristol, Southampton, London, Amsterdam, La Rochelle, Nantes, Lisbon, Boston, Charleston who financed and manned the fleets that transported Africans across the Atlantic, and with African chiefs and Arab raiders who worked with the European in a partnership that originated with European demands. The trade linked together African village people in scattered forest districts who were suddenly attacked and carried off or killed, slaves in the great market at Whydah, slaves in the barraccoons at Calabar, sugar planters in the West Indies, cotton and tobacco planters in Virginia and the Carolinas, plantation owners around Bahia, soldiers from the armies of England and France dying by the score in the islands, Maroons in the mountains of Jamaica, black men in Haiti winning their freedom.

The African who arrived in the island had already survived two terrifying experiences. One was the physical shock of capture, confinement, sale, and of a long sea voyage under conditions of indescribable hardship. The other was the more severe psychological shock of being torn from family, kinsmen, the familiar supporting structure of the tribe and the protection of ancestral spirits and of being completely at the mercy of men so different in colour and in culture, and of being removed from the firm earth that was the basis of life to the huge rolling ocean. This drove men mad, sent them leaping to their death from the decks of the slave ships or rising in hopeless mutiny.

The importation of Africans increased from year to year, Jamaica alone taking 610,000 between 1700 and 1786,[56] and each cargo load of bewildered slaves delivered in the West Indies gave a new shape to West Indian society and a new direction to the history of the island communities.

5   War and Trade: 1650–1834

IN 1650 THE BRITISH EMPIRE in the Caribbean was the size of the Isle of Man and Anglesey. It was increased tenfold by the capture of Jamaica in 1655. The island was the first English colony to be taken by force and the first Spanish colony to be lost in this way. At the time of its conquest it had a population of about 5,000. The Arawaks had been wiped out. The inhabitants consisted of Spanish farmers and Negro slaves who grew cassava and maize, raised cattle and horses, and traded with passing ships as well as with Cuba and the Spanish Main.

The island was taken as an afterthought by Penn and Venables, following on their disgraceful failure at Santo Domingo, but it was nevertheless of great value. The first to realize this were English buc-caneers who shared Tortuga with French filibusters, and who increas-ingly found French rule irksome. Having sharp eyes for plunder, and noting that the island lay in the very belly of all commerce, they moved from their fortress rock off the northwest coast of Hispaniola to Port Royal, at the end of the 7-mile arm of land that almost encloses Kingston Harbour. Within ten years they transformed this sandy cactus-covered tip of land into a boisterous base, well on its way to becoming one of the richest towns in the New World. This was the base from which Mansfelt and Morgan set out to 'gall the Spaniards on every side'. To such an extent did buccaneering be-come everyman's business that a Governor described it as the sick-ness of Jamaica.[57] Changes in English policy, prompted by a desire 'to force trade with Spain', and the recognition that piracy kills trade, led to the suppression of the buccaneers. Yet their presence had been of benefit to the island, for their destructive raids on Spanish cities and their reputation for ferocity protected the infant colony of Jamaica from a Spanish counter-attack, and the silver and gold that poured into Port Royal provided needed capital for planting and for trade.

Behind a screen of buccaneering sloops, settlers began to move into the island. Cromwell ordered that young men and women from Ireland and vagrants from Scotland should be sent out to Jamaica, and he saw to it that the island received a supply of settlers. Modyford and some planters who moved with him from Barbados introduced sugar technology and began to produce sugar. Before long sugar plantations were spreading across the savannahs of Vere in the south of Jamaica, and along the fertile strip of coastal plain around Montego Bay on the north coast. The old names are still remembered, the Barretts of Cinnamon Hill, the Halls of Tryall, the Stirlings of Content, the Lawrences of Running Gut.

The method of cultivation was the same as in Barbados and the Leeward Islands. It was marked by the ruthless exploitation of virgin land and by a fall in sugar production as the soil became exhausted. Barbados began by being land-rich. As it was small it showed signs of becoming land-poor by 1700. In Nevis the production of sugar began to decline early because the covering of soil was thin, and the rocky bones of the land were soon exposed. Jamaica in 1700 had ample reserves of virgin land. It moved into the lead, becoming by 1750 the giant among the sugar-producing islands, with a white population of 10,000 and 130,000 slaves; but when the French began to develop Sainte Domingue the familiar story was repeated and the colony with the largest reserves of virgin land out-produced the others.

By 1700 it was abundantly clear that islands heavily engaged in sugar production and in buying slaves were extremely valuable, and that the slave trade was worth the lives of many thousands, being 'the very mainspring of the machine that sets in motion all the other wheels',[58] so the Caribbean became one of the main areas of conflict between the powers of Europe. In the 113 years between 1702 and 1815 five major wars were fought, covering a period of 56 years, and in all these the islands were closely involved.

No transfer of territory resulted from the War of the Spanish Succession which broke out in 1702. England entered the war in order
to keep Louis XIV and members of his family off the Spanish
throne, and to prevent the Spanish Empire in Europe and in the
Americas from falling under the dominance of France. The chief
battles were fought in Europe, but both France and England sent
fleets to the Caribbean. St Kitts and Nevis suffered heavily. In each
of these islands life still had the character of that in a frontier town,
with a large measure of insecurity because of raids by the Spanish and
French and the prevalence of privateers who, said a planter, 'were so
thick among the islands that we can't sail from island to island but
with more hazard than between England and this place'.[59] The
houses of the planters were rudely built, with roofs of thatch, floors
of brick and walls of mountain timber. Planters and even the
Governor took a hand in trade, often turning a dishonest penny by
fitting out a privateer, or by smuggling. An official investigator found
that Dutch ships had the practice of stopping at St Kitts on their way
from Holland under the pretext of watering, and that the captains
took the opportunity of contriving with the local planters to smuggle
goods ashore.

After the ships reached Statia they sent back long boats for water,
though one boatload would have lasted for a month; and the boats
returned with sugar that should have gone to the agents and creditors
of the planters in England.[60] The gentry, factious and envious of
each other, had a reputation for over-eating, and for drunkenness.
They complained bitterly that England left them without protection
and at the same time the Assembly in Nevis refused to billet soldiers
unless they worked with the Negroes in the fields so as to earn their
keep. One planter expressed the generally contentious colonial attitude when he objected to billeting, saying that there was no law in
England for quartering soldiers and that he would consign the
King's orders to an unmentionable place.[61] But he and his fellows
knew the bitterness of invasion when Iberville invaded St Kitts and
Nevis in 1706, burning the dwelling-houses and boiling-houses, and
carrying off slaves, horses and food as well as the sugar mills and
coppers.

By the Treaty of Utrecht in 1713 Spain granted to England the right to send one ship a year to the Plate, and, far more important, the prized Asiento, an agreement that England would supply slaves to the Spanish colonies in America. Jamaica now became a great centre for trade. The English slave ships took their cargoes of Africans to Kingston and to Montego Bay for sale locally and for re-export to Spanish America. At this time the annual importation was at the rate of about 15,000 a year, about two-thirds of this total being re-exported. This trade in men and women was extremely lucrative. One merchant is reported to have sent back in one year £50,000 for slaves he sold in Montego Bay.[62]

Alongside the legal trade there was a profitable illicit trade. The Governors of Jamaica encouraged log-wood cutters who settled in Yucatan and around the Belize River territory and shipped logwood to Jamaica. They camped in territory claimed by Spain. Out of one of these scattered settlements originated the colony of British Honduras. Kingston was also a base for smugglers who slipped out of the harbour with supplies of English manufactured goods for sale to Spanish colonists, returning with indigo and other dye woods, hides and cochineal. The Spanish American trade was highly prized by England and the North American colonies since from it they obtained much-needed currency for coping with their balance of payments problem. In order to get as much Spanish silver as possible England made Kingston and Falmouth free ports in 1766. This enabled Spaniards to buy slaves and manufactured goods in both these ports, paying for them in their own currency.

The illicit trade was an offence against Spain's authority and her naval patrols often acted with undue severity against those whom they caught. A result of this festering irritation was war, which broke out in 1739, the last item in a long list of English grievances and complaints about Spanish inhumanity being the severed ear of Captain Jenkins. But England's chief rival for empire was now France. She entered the war on the side of Spain in 1744. Since the English colonies produced sugar at a higher cost than the French colonies the English set out to wreck the French sugar plantations and disrupt their trade. They might have succeeded in their strategy of strip and starve but for the fact that the Yankee traders, putting profits before patriotism, continued to trade with the French colonies; so in the Caribbean the old colonial system showed cracks and cleavages.

In the war of 1756, under Pitt's leadership, the strategy was that of taking France's colonies from her in every part of the world. Because the English navy won command of the Caribbean, the English took Martinique, Guadeloupe and Cuba, and occupied the four neutral islands of Dominica, Tobago, St Vincent and St Lucia. By the Peace of 1763 England kept Grenada and all the neutral islands but gave up Cuba and Guadeloupe.

In this way three of the four Windward Islands became English colonies. Dominica, Grenada and St Vincent, unlike low-lying Barbados and Antigua, have towering forest-clad mountains. The absence of flat land saved them from the dominance of sugar. They were settled by small and middling French farmers who lived on their estates and holdings, cultivating cacao, cotton and coffee. Only a small quantity of sugar was produced. Whereas the Leeward Islands are predominantly Protestant, the Windwards are chiefly Roman Catholic. Many of the peasants still speak a French patois, so that they can communicate with a peasant from Martinique or Haiti but not with one from Barbados or Antigua since he speaks a creole language based on English. The creole culture of the English colonies, based on African slavery, the plantation and miscegenation, is filtered through England in the Leeward Islands, but in the Windward Islands it is filtered through France as well as England.

The war of 1776 was quite different from the earlier ones. It was the first war of independence to be waged in the New World in the period of European expansion. It was also the first successful rising of a colonial people in modern times. The Haitian war of Independence followed, but it differed in being the rising by a slave population and not of free men, of Africans and not people of European descent. After the establishment of Haitian independence there followed wars of liberation in South and Central America. Cuba fought its war of independence at the end of the nineteenth century.

48

The West India planters and colonists had grievances similar to those of the North Americans. Self-interest taught them that they were dependent on New England for food and plantation supplies and from earlier experience they knew that if the shipping lines were cut the plantations would languish, and slaves and free men would die from hunger. They were therefore anxious to prevent the outbreak of war between England and her American colonies. But they were at many points in agreement with the Americans. They resented taxation without representation, and some West Indians rioted against the Stamp Duties.[63] Like the Americans, they had representative government without responsible government. They too found control from London irksome and many of the restrictions put on them intolerably irritating. But they decided in the end to stand with Britain. One reason for resisting the persuasions of the North Americans was that they knew they had to depend on England for defence and for markets. Another reason was that there were no West Indians in the sense that there were Americans. The West India planters were Englishmen who identified themselves with England, their home. It was in England that the most effective leaders of the West India interest resided. Those Englishmen who resided in the West Indies were masters in a slave community in which they were heavily outnumbered and of which they kept control by repressive and harsh laws. Liberty, Justice and Independence were words that they could not invoke. Nor had they the will to act together as one people or nation, such as was found in America.

In 1774 the Continental Congress closed its ports to goods from the West Indies and in 1775 it stopped exportation to the islands. The price of sugar rose on the London market but the high price had its disadvantages, leading as it did to a demand for the importation of a larger quantity of cheaper sugar from foreign countries.[64] The planters had foreseen famine, and by 1776 there were severe shortages of foodstuffs in Barbados and the Leeward Islands. The danger of invasion was added to that of famine when France entered the war against England in 1778. Dominica fell to the French, but England took St Lucia. The French re-took St Lucia and captured St Vincent, Grenada, Tobago, and St Kitts. An attack on Jamaica was only prevented by Rodney's defeat of the French fleet at The Saintes off Guadeloupe. By the Peace of 1784 England regained Grenada, St Vincent, St Kitts, Montserrat, Nevis and Dominica, but St Lucia and Tobago remained with France. It was the fate of the eastern islands to be fragmented and tossed about. Had they been left as one large group with either England or France they would have been more viable and have had a greater chance of unity.

Groans and cries went up from the West India planters and merchants, with urgent pleadings that the return of peace should mark a return to normal in the trade with North America. The West India interest used all its power to influence Parliament, but failed. The United States was now a foreign state, and restrictions were put on trade between the English colonies and those now independent. In the islands prices went up and the encumbrances and debts on plantations increased. The failure of the powerful West India interest is significant. The time of sunset was drawing near.

The high cost of sugar production in the English colonies now began to tell against them. St Domingue was outproducing them. Its sugar cost was a fifth less, its average yield five times better than that of Jamaica, where some plantations were going out of production.[65] The English islands had been first off the mark, but the French colonies had overtaken and passed them. Just as all had marvelled at the speed with which Jamaica forged forward in the 1750s so now the world marvelled at the productivity and wealth of St Domingue.

There were other competitors beyond the Caribbean. In 1789 the East India Company decided to turn its attention to sugar production.[66] In Europe the pressures of revolution and change were building up fast, and the swift increase that took place in trade between Britain and the United States in the six years between 1784 and 1790 indicated that the old mercantilist theories were out of date. How would the almost static economy of the West Indies fare in a world of revolutionary change, in which steam power was displacing muscle power, and freedom was becoming a watchword?

The French Revolutionary and Napoleonic Wars lasted from 1793 to 1815, with a brief breathing space in 1802. Nelson's victory at Trafalgar freed the islands from fear of invasion. In 1815 the Treaty of Paris added the islands of St Lucia, Tobago and Trinidad to the British West Indies.

At the time of its capture from Spain in 1798 Trinidad had a population of 17,643.[67] Of this number 10,000 were Negroes. The island was short of labour and remained so until the importation of East Indian indentured labourers got under way in the middle of the nineteenth century. Only then did Trinidad become a sugar plantation island.

The contrast between Jamaica at the start of the eighteenth century and Trinidad at its close illumines the change in world opinion. In 1700 Jamaica was importing large numbers of African slaves, and the English government's achievement in securing an Asiento in 1713 for the supply of slaves to Spanish America was the envy of other European nations. A century later, in 1802, Canning declared that any attempt to import into Trinidad enough Negro slaves to develop its sugar plantations would appal the feelings of every member of the House of Commons.[68] In 1792 the Danish king forbade his subjects to buy, sell or transport slaves. In 1807 the English Parliament abolished slave trade.

In the period of slavery Jamaica and the older English colonies had representative but not responsible government. There was an elected element in their Legislature, but on a very restricted franchise. The Assemblies, elected on a narrow franchise, were representative only of a small segment of the population. They were not concerned with reform but with preserving vested interests. The number of these Assemblies was increased by the acquisition of the Windward Islands in 1763. The first plan had been to have one Governor-General and one Legislature in these islands but each island insisted on having its own.[69] The conquest of Trinidad raised the question as to what system of government should be introduced. The old representative system had proved completely unsatisfactory; but this did not mean that an elected system would not work. What the English government did was to abandon both the old representative system and the principle of an elected element in the legislature. Trinidad was made a Crown Colony, under a Governor appointed from London, who governed with the advice of a Legislative Council to which he named all the members.

Two dates mark the end of the old system of labour and of the protective duties that West Indian sugar had enjoyed under the old colonial system. In 1834 all slaves in British territories were set free. In 1845 the protective duties that shielded West Indian sugar from foreign competition were withdrawn.

6   A Race Set Free

THERE ARE THREE WATERSHED DATES in the history of the West Indies. They are points of no return, brief periods when the gathering forces of change gained the upper hand and new directions and new goals were set.

The first of these decisive dates is 1650 when it became clear that sugar would take possession of Barbados, displacing tobacco, with the estate owner dispossessing the smallholder and the African slave the white bondservant. The second is 1834 when the British Parliament enforced an Act of Emancipation that put an end to slavery in British colonial territories and removed the foundation on which the old plantation economy was based. The third covers the years from 1938 to 1944, marking the end of the post-emancipation period of colonial rule and the establishment of popular governments through universal adult suffrage, with independence and nationhood as accepted goals.[70]

New directions were set in each of these periods but traces of the old attitudes, values and stereotypes did not suddenly and miraculously disappear. The master-slave relationship continued for generations after 1834. The colonial attitude and the image of the metropole remained after 1944. The white-coloured-black system of status ranking, the stereotypes and self-concepts, the value-judgements and psychological tensions were carried over from the period of slavery into the post-emancipation period and, in diminishing degree, into the present. A race was freed in 1834 and it became necessary to create a society.[71] No people can do this for any other people. The task is being undertaken now by the independent West Indian governments.

The social organization that existed at the time of emancipation had been developed over a century and a half. It was rigidly hierarchical, built up of the three layers of white, brown and black arranged in pyramidal form, with a comparatively small apex of whites and a large base of black and coloured slaves. Although these three groups were clearly differentiated they were all essential parts of a society organized to produce sugar. A West Indian anthropologist has described the groups as differing

'in their religious observances and concepts, their legal and political institutions, education, kinship and mating patterns, family organization, property rights, land tenure and use, division of labour, language, occupations and technology, community organization and associations, markets, valuesystems, recreation and folklore . . . a society divided into sections, each of which practised different cultures'.[72]

The differences in status and occupation were marked clearly, visibly, in colour.

The whites formed the apex of the pyramid, at the very top being large proprietors and senior officials, and below them white employees, estate bookkeepers, master tradesmen and the like. Whiteness was a symbol of freedom and of status, for this group held all positions of control and power. Through the old system of representative government based on a narrow franchise requiring property qualifications, the whites controlled the making of laws, and through their control of the militia and courts they controlled the enforcement of the law. Through their ownership of land and of the means of production, including the slave, they had complete economic power.

It was characteristic of the most important of the owners and officials that they were absentees. Edward Long, one of the most distinguished of the creole historians of the period, whose *History of Jamaica* was published in 1774, complained bitterly about the patent offices, by which patentees in England, 'Aegyptian task masters',[73] farmed out their offices to lesser men, and annually collected their 'several thousand pounds'. Ecclesiastics farmed out benefices to priests of doubtful character, such as the Rev. Audain who left his religious duties for two years in order to go privateering.[74]

Absenteeism was a sign of success. The metropole was home. By 1800 absenteeism was widespread through the older sugar islands. In 1830 a Colonial Office official remarked of the West Indies that there was no civilized society on earth

'so entirely destitute of learned leisure, of literary and scientific intercourse, and even of liberal occupations. Perhaps it would be difficult to find a white man in the island of Jamaica who does not regard England as his home and the Colony as his place of Exile'.[75]

Absenteeism was linked also with an absence from West Indian society of white women, and of home life. Children were, as a rule, sent to school in England. Concubinage was general. Planters of consequence manumitted their coloured children. It was a disgrace for them not to do so. White men of lesser station usually had neither the means nor the authority to free their children. Illegitimacy in the white West Indian context was of no consequence.[76]

An absentee proprietor operated his property through an attorney; and since the attorney usually had in his care a number of properties he managed each through an overseer, in whose hands rested immense authority. The two people most concerned with the ownership and good management of the estate lived away from it for much of the time.

There are, in the islands, gracious buildings that indicate what a resident aristocracy might have achieved. Some charming Georgian houses that survive in Basseterre in St Kitts, overlooking a small square called Pall Mall, the Palladian window in the church at Parham in Antigua, some of the old country houses in Barbados, the square in Spanish Town in Jamaica and some of the Jamaican Great Houses all have distinction.[77] But essentially West Indian society was grossly materialistic and sordid.

Fear was ever-present. The whites were few in number, the blacks many: 'hence came insecurity, insecurity bred fear, and fear bred cruelty'.[78] The fear was intensified by the Negro's persistent resistance to slavery, and even more by the rising in Haiti. Great houses were built as forts. Risings were put down with the greatest severity, as in Montego Bay in 1831. This alarmist attitude led the West Indian Assemblies to resist every attempt from London to ameliorate the condition of the slaves, since these were interpreted as threats to the power structure. The humanitarians who campaigned against slavery turned away from the local Assemblies and identified liberalism with paternalist government from Whitehall.[79]

The whites were, in fact, trapped in the rigid society they had established. In his analysis of the effects of slavery in the West Indies Lucas concluded that, even if 'under certain extraordinary circumstances it may be good for a man to be a slave, it is not conceivable that under any circumstances it can be good for a man to be a slave-holder'.[80] Slavery degraded both the owner and the owned, and straight-jacketed him so that he could not introduce the innovations and new techniques on which his own society depended. White society exhibited a deep-seated psychological insecurity, an extreme sensitivity about status and titles, the assumption of superiority on the grounds of colour and an authoritarian attitude.

Free coloured and black people made up the second tier in the pyramid. Like the whites, they were free; unlike them, their rights as citizens were limited. They were debarred from voting, holding seats in the legislature, managing estates, inheriting property of more than a certain value, giving evidence in a court of law against a white man. Many of them owned property, including slaves, and they had a reputation for being inconsiderate and cruel masters.[81] Their social advancement rested on the extent to which they could become 'white' so they tended to marry persons lighter in colour, to imitate the whites and despise the black.

Yet, in spite of its snobbery and jealousies, this was a West Indian group, with its roots in the islands and not in England.

The country offered to this group little opportunity for advancement. Some ran small plantations with a few slaves, but their status as free men debarred them from agricultural labour, which was slave's work. Most of them moved to the towns, where they worked in junior supervisory jobs, hired out jobbing gangs of slaves, became apprentices to lawyers and business men, educated themselves, took an interest in books and ideas, became journalists and printers and agitated for the abolition of civil disabilities. Rejected by the whites, they finally took up the cause of the slave. In Jamaica coloured leaders like Edward Jordon, Robert Osborn, Richard Hill and William George Gordon spearheaded the assault on civil dis/ abilities and slavery.[82] From this group emerged the West Indian middle/class of the post/emancipation period.

The slaves, the largest group in the population, the 'sinews of the plantation',[83] were the base on which rested the whole West Indian economy. Among them also there were differences of status, the creole slave considering himself superior to the immigrant, the coloured to the black, the household slave to the field slave. The highest status rested with those who exercised authority, the driver in the field, the 'chief governor' in the sugar works, the headman in the cattle pen.

The West Indian system of slavery reduced the slave to the status of property, of being a thing, a piece of equipment or stock, like the cattle and mules. But 'the slave had also a social status and a capacity to organize and to provide for himself if the opportunity were allowed'.[84] He was both property and person, livestock and man, and for that reason the slave/system itself, in practice, underwent modifications and relaxations between 1650 and 1834.

One of the most important of these was the right to a 'provision ground'. The Consolidated Slave Acts provided for allowances of specified imported foods and clothing, farm tools, the use of food grown around the slave cottage or on provision grounds, the right to every Sunday and every other Saturday for cultivating his food. In many instances slaves were allowed to keep livestock. They sold their produce, kept the profits from their own trading, and so owned a certain amount of property. Since the estate also provided hospital care, many slaves in the latter part of the period of slavery had greater security than some of the free blacks and coloureds.

As the number of slaves increased the provision of food became a major problem. In some islands, especially in Jamaica, the chief

English sugar-producing island in the eighteenth century, the slaves were allowed to cultivate food crops on marginal land, often in the foothills near the estate. The provision ground complemented the plantation, providing locally grown food, and so reducing the dependence on imported food. The provision grounds in the more mountainous islands like Jamaica and Haiti prepared the way for the independent peasantry of the present day, and for the marketing system which the slave, and later the peasant, obtained, almost a complete monopoly of the supply of root-crops. Some islands, like Barbados and St Kitts, were wholly sugar islands. These obtained some of their food from nearby islands that were more mountainous: St Kitts from Nevis, Barbados from Dominica and St Vincent.

The Negro brought to the West Indies many elements of the culture of a large number of African peoples, the Shango religion of the Yorubas, Vodun, which is the Dahomey term for all deities, the Spider-tales of the Ashanti Akan people, proverbs, words, snatches of music. But coming as a captive into a strange society where another culture was dominant, he had to discard his own social conventions and institutions and his concept of his own value.

The most terrible deprivations that he had to endure were not those of the body but of the personality. As an example, plantation slavery destroyed the role of the father. The African came from an organized tribal society with its carefully regulated codes and conventions into one where the male begat children who became the master's property; and it was the master, not the father, who had the natural obligation to protect, provide, educate, demand respect, exercise authority.[85] Marriage had no place in this society, parenthood was limited – for the man – to procreation, mating was unstable, and the child was neither legitimate nor illegitimate, but a piece of property. If, therefore, after emancipation, for various reasons the majority of the slaves and their descendants continued to mate in unstable associations lacking legal recognition, the 'illegitimate status of the children had no significance among them'.[86]

Another example of the damage done to the personality lay in the fact that many slaves came to accept the 'planter-image' of themselves as inferior beings, of the Negro as slave or labourer, of authority and power and worth as being European attributes.

On the other hand, the West Indies have a long tradition of slave risings and rebellions. The Maroons of Jamaica originated with African slaves who retreated into the mountains when the English took the island. Some accepted offers of land and settled down. Others refused, and their numbers were augmented from time to time by runaway slaves. They fought a guerrilla war against the Government of Jamaica for 78 years, until their freedom and independence as a community was recognized by treaty in 1738. They, and the Haitian slaves, are the two groups that achieved independence by force of arms.

In the years following 1800 the slaves became increasingly restive. They knew of the Haitian rising and of the victories of Toussaint. There were at work among them missionaries from whom they must have learned of the efforts of Wilberforce and Clarkson. Their masters were subject to continual attacks for inefficiency and wastefulness from economists like Adam Smith and from the new sugar-producing countries like Cuba, Mauritius and the East Indies. In defence, the legislature of the Leeward Islands declared that 'no power shall endeavour to deprive us of obtaining slaves from Africa'.[87]

The slave owners were given a breathing-space through the outbreak of the French Revolution and the long-drawn out Napoleonic Wars. Wilberforce estimated a delay of four years. It turned out to be 15. Year after year he moved his resolution that the Slave Trade should be abolished, coming to the very edge of success when in 1803 the Bill passed the House of Commons. It was thrown out by the House of Lords. Finally, in 1807, it passed both Houses and became law in 1808.

This ended the British Slave Trade. Other nations carried on the trade up to 1865. In the Caribbean Cuba took large quantities of slaves. But in the West Indies the struggle slowly became one for emancipation. The West India interest, once powerful, now impoverished, was discredited as being inefficient and inhumane.

Pressure built up in England in favour of emancipation through the leadership of Wilberforce and Buxton. In the West Indies some missionaries conformist at first were forced by conscience and circumstance to take a stand against slavery. The free coloured at first kept aloof from the anti-slavery campaign, then joined in the attack. The slaves rose in Guiana in 1823 and in 1832 they rebelled in Jamaica, thinking that freedom had been granted but was being deliberately withheld. Pressure from without the West Indies and from within, agitation, mutiny, political and economic pressure all contributed to the Act of Emancipation.

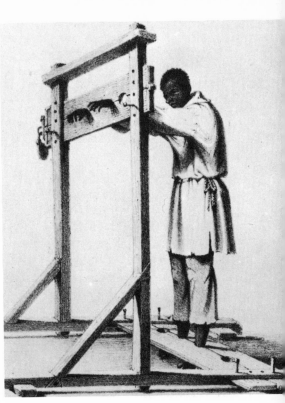

18, 19, 20 Punishments inflicted in the sugar-and-slave plantation period on the Negro population. (*above*) The punishment for over-eating and drinking. (*right and below*) Two other forms of punishment for petty offences.

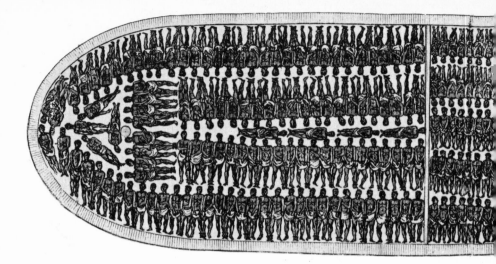

21 During the seventeenth and eighteenth centuries large numbers of Africans were imported into the West Indies to work as slaves on the sugar plantations. This is a plan of a slave-ship.

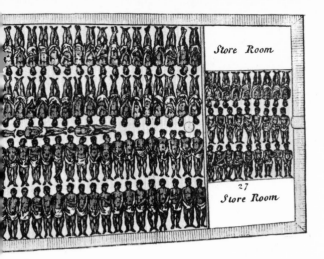

Store Room

27
Store Room

22 (*below far left*) Josiah Wedgwood, one of the many anti-slavery campaigners, designed this cameo to try and gain support for his cause.

23, 24 (*below, left and right*) A little-known figure in the rejection of slavery was Three-Fingered Jack, a run-away slave and highwayman, who was killed in a fight with a Maroon, Quashee.

25 The old system of representative government was oligarchic and inefficient. In Jamaica discontent came to a head in the Morant Bay rising, led by a Baptist deacon, Paul Bogle.

26 Government in the West Indies was based on British institutions. This drawing of a law court dates from the early nineteenth century.

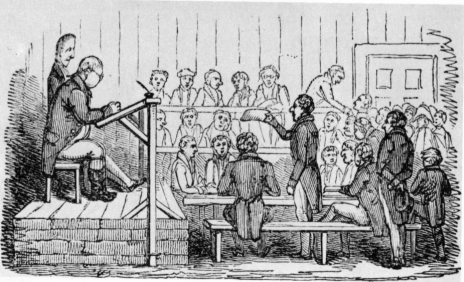

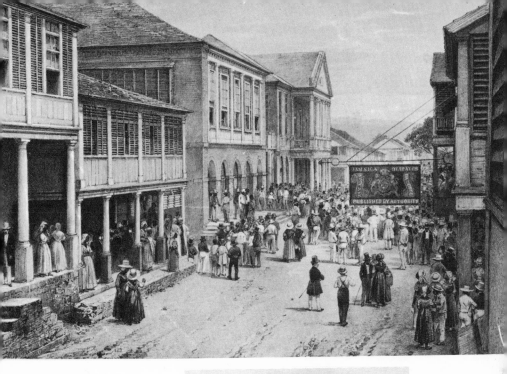

27 In Jamaica before 1865 and in Barbados, through a limited franchise, power was in the hands of the white merchants and planters. Outside the courthouse on Election day in Kingston, Jamaica, from a nineteenth-century engraving.

28 Government by a majority Negro population was not realized until 1944. The insistence by the Negro leader Marcus Garvey (1887–1940) on the dignity and equality of the Negro assisted in bringing about radical social changes throughout the West Indies.

29, 30, 31 Three of the most significant West Indian leaders of the nineteenth century who aimed for the advance of the Negro were George William Gordon (*above left*), Richard Hill (*above*) and Robert Osborn. They were among the first coloured West Indian intellectuals.

32 The social habits and attitudes of Jamaica are realistically reflected in the nineteenth-century paintings of James Hakewill. This is King Street, Jamaica.

33 This early nineteenth-century engraving is entitled 'Sunday Morning in Town'. Some free coloured people owned property and kept slaves.

34 Montego Bay, now a famous tourist resort, early became a busy sugar port.

35 St George's harbour, Grenada, is one of the most beautiful harbours in the Eastern Caribbean. Cocoa, nutmegs and bananas are the island's chief exports.

7   The Crown in Control : 1834–1944

THE REVOLUTION that took place in 1834 was incomplete. The Act of Emancipation put an end to slavery as an institution and changed the legal status of nine-tenths of the population of the West Indies, but it also provided that the newly freed people should continue to serve their masters as apprentices for six more years. Slavery, therefore, was continued in the form of forced labour, 'the Negroes having to work as slaves for so many hours a week'.[88] Antigua dispensed with the period of apprenticeship but the other islands attempted to enforce it. The system provoked such strong resentment that it was abandoned in 1838, two years before the prescribed time.

Up to this point West Indian society had rested on the slave-and-sugar estate, conceived as a social and economic unit in which the master and the slave each had certain obligations; the slave to work under direction at the production of sugar for export and at growing food crops for subsistence; the master to direct, regulate, and to provide food, clothing and medical services. The effective labour force was maintained at the required strength by the purchase of new slaves. The estate owner dealt through an English agent who sold his sugar and bought his supplies for him. If supplies were purchased through the agent who received the crop

'they could be largely transformed from a cash transaction to a book entry to be offset against the proceeds of the sugar crop. . . . One of the leading characteristics of the sugar industry under slavery was its extreme economy of working capital.'[89]

The abolition of the slave trade in 1807 made it difficult, if not impossible, for the planter to keep his effective labour force up to

69

strength, since he could no longer import slaves. In Trinidad, especially, the planter attempted to overcome this difficulty by importing slaves from the nearby islands, using every subterfuge and trick that could be devised.[90]

Emancipation changed radically the whole basis of social organization by making the slave a free man, with the power to sell or to withhold his labour, to remain on the estate or to move away from the estate. His labour had to be bought, and for this labour the planter had to pay cash. The whole labour cost of the estate was put on to a cash basis and the relationship between master and slave changed into one between employer and employee, but it took more than a century for the new status of the worker to be accepted.

The revolution of the 1830s was also incomplete because it left untouched the constitutional framework that had protected and buttressed plantation slavery. The political power that enforced the revolution came from the Imperial Parliament which passed the Act of Emancipation in the face of determined opposition from the colonial legislatures. Each island Assembly claimed that Westminster had no power to legislate for its own internal affairs; yet it was left to these factious Assemblies, representative almost wholly of planter interests, to direct the course of freedom. The revolution 'was an anomaly among revolutions . . . the political power that enforced the revolution was withdrawn . . . the ruling minority found itself in control of a revolution it had not made and did not want'.[91]

This was true of all the colonies except Trinidad. There the Crown was fully in control. The island, taken from Spain by conquest in 1798, had been neglected up to 1783. In that year it had a population of 126 white persons, 295 coloured and 310 slaves, whereas Jamaica then had a population of 25,000 whites and just over 210,000 slaves. The British government, finding the West Indian Houses of Assembly intolerably difficult and refractory, decided not to establish the old type of colonial constitution in Trinidad. Also, it had no confidence in the ability of the coloured people of the island, who were in the majority.[92] Many of them had been brought up under French rule. Without attempting the experiment of seeing if they could make representative government work it threw

70

the representational principle overboard and put the island under a Governor responsible only to London. The West Indian tradition of authoritarianism was retained with this change, that it was main/ tained not by a local planter oligarchy but by the metropolitan power.

At the time of emancipation the population structure of Trinidad was very different from that of the other English colonies. The pro/ portion of freemen to slaves was of the order of one to one, as against one to ten in the other islands. Barbados had become a plantation island in the seventeenth century with the aid of African slaves. Jamaica became a sugar/and/slave island at the beginning of the eighteenth century. Trinidad was not yet a plantation island in 1834. It could have become an island of smallholders with a diversified agriculture. But sugar was king. The sugar plantation could yield profits if labour were abundant and cheap. With the backing of the Imperial government and financed by public funds the Trinidad planters followed the example of Mauritius and turned to India for the labour they needed. East Indian immigration reached massive figures. Between 1838 and 1917 nearly half a million Indians were imported into the Caribbean, about 145,000 of them into Trinidad, 21,500 into Jamaica, and more than a quarter million into what was then British Guiana and is now Guyana.

The East Indians were brought in as indentured labourers, each one under contract to work for a particular estate for five years. Since Britain had abandoned its old policy of protection for West Indian products in the home market in 1846, West Indian sugar had to compete with world sugar, and this it could do only by keeping its labour costs low. A Trinidad Ordnance of July 1899 indicates what this meant. It ordered that the working day should be nine hours, less half an hour for lunch, at not less than 25 cents a day for an able/ bodied adult. Accommodation had to be provided, not less than 50 feet of superficial space for an adult; also medical care. A Trini/ dadian reviewing the system of indentured East Indian labour for a Royal Commission in 1897 came to the conclusion that

'with regard to its effect on the employer the system is not very different from slavery, with the gaol substituted for the whip. And

one of the worst consequences of Indian immigration into Trinidad has been to keep its educated class at the moral level of slave
owners.'[93]

In this way, with the help of the East Indians, Trinidad became a
sugar plantation colony. Its sugar exports increased five-fold but at
the price of: 'semi-servitude, sub-human wages, the degradation of
labour and the perpetuation of the Crown Colony system of
government'.[94]

Among the East Indian immigrants the mortality rate was high.
Life in the barracks was unhealthy. Typhoid and tuberculosis were
rampant. Thrifty and hardworking, devoted to their families, ambi-
tious, those who survived very soon saw that their security rested in
the ownership of land. They saved money and they bought property.
'In the social sense the outstanding result of indentured Indian immigration was the emergence for the first time in the history of Trinidad of a class of small farmers.'[95]

A century earlier exactly the same process had begun to take place
in Jamaica. Where there was no available land it could not happen.
Barbados provides an example of the way in which the lack of land
put the worker at the mercy of the planter. As late as 1872 the average
annual wage of a sugar worker was estimated at about £5. This wage
was subject to fines and deductions at will. 'Located labourers'
occupied houses on the estate for which they paid rent. All workers
were subject to a Masters and Servants Act of 1840 which in its
operation reduced the free labourer to serfdom of the most iniquitous
kind. A man could be ejected at four weeks' notice and his growing
crop taken over at an appraised value.[96] The Poor House and Gaol
were used as instruments of punishment. The black worker learned
that to be secure it was necessary to conform; but the appearance of
conformity masked deep bitter resentments.

The attitude of the Jamaica planter class was the same as that in
Barbados, or in Mississippi or Alabama in the twentieth century.
They did not accept the implications of Emancipation. The Jamaica
legislature was more difficult and rebellious, so much so that a
Governor, who had been transferred from Barbados to Jamaica, came

to the conclusion that the Assembly was insane, and gave up all hope of persuading it to co-operate in establishing better conditions for freedom. He reported to London that as far as obedience to the laws and commands of the Sovereign went the white population were in actual rebellion, and that the whole generation of those who had held authority under slavery would have to die before there could be any material improvement.

The planter was in fact desperate. His estate was heavily encumbered or mortgaged, and much of the compensation paid to him for his slaves had gone to his creditors. The failure of local banks in 1838 and the collapse of a number of West Indian houses in England in 1846 occurred at the period when he needed capital to pay his labourers and put in new equipment in place of the obsolete factory machinery that had sufficed under a system of protection. But capital was hard to get. Jamaica no longer attracted investors. Most absentee owners sold out and invested their money elsewhere. The removal of the protective duties in 1846 completed the ruin. Sugar production declined from 1,431,689 cwt in 1832 to 511,247 cwt in 1852. Coffee production fell from 17·7 million lbs in 1834 to 4 million lbs in 1849. In that year the production of ginger was a fourth what it had been between 1825 and 1839. Owners went bankrupt, estates were abandoned or sold out, and the number of white persons in the island dropped from 15,775 in 1844 to 13,815 in 1861.

The decline of the plantation came about chiefly because of a breakdown in relationships between the planter who persisted in trying to coerce labour and the worker who was not prepared to accept terms that denied him his freedom. One estimate puts the number of workers who left the plantations at 50 per cent of the effective labour force. The number of freehold properties increased, rising from 2,014 in 1838 to 7,848 in 1840. The decision to move must have been difficult, for it meant leaving the estate community, the slave cottage and provision ground for backlands or hilly country. Some labourers set up free villages under the leadership of Baptist and Methodist missionaries, and cultivated root crops for food and for sale. Sir Charles Metcalfe, while Governor of Jamaica, put the problem bluntly:

'It naturally became the interest of the owners of properties to obtain labour on the cheapest, and that of the labouring population to sell it on the dearest terms; and a struggle between these opposite views commenced between the two parties.'[97]

To many people the movement from the estates seemed calamitous, for it was on the estate that the prosperity of the West Indies had always depended. This was the view of many officials as well as planters. Lord Grey, who was Secretary of State for the Colonies, advocated a heavy tax on peasant produce so as to make work on the estates more profitable; and in Trinidad a rule was made that no Crown Land should be sold in lots of less than 100 acres.[98]

This wish to limit the peasants was one reason why the Jamaica House of Assembly was slow to take over from the estates the obligation to provide public services. Besides, the island was almost bankrupt. It had no Civil Service. Its road system was bad. There was a general shortage of cash. The local administration of justice broke down, for the Vestry was dominated by the planter, and as in Barbados every advantage was taken of the peasant. In the 1860s three years of drought added to the general misery. Food crops perished and discontent grew. It came to a head in Morant Bay, the capital of one of the country parishes of Jamaica, where there was a clash between 400 small settlers under a Baptist Deacon, Paul Bogle, and the Custos and Vestry of the Parish. The Riot Act was read, stones were thrown, the militia fired on the crowd. Twenty-one white persons and nine Negro rioters were killed. In the suppression that followed, 439 persons were killed, 1,000 Negro houses burned, 600 people flogged[99]. Panic-stricken at its inadequacy, the House of Assembly passed an Act abolishing itself.

The decline of the Jamaica sugar estates and the decision of the Assembly to abolish itself carried further in Jamaica the revolution that began with emancipation. The rising at Morant Bay was in no sense a rebellion. It was an outburst provoked by many causes, such as the breakdown of the administration of justice through the local magistracy, poverty for which there seemed to be no remedy, three years of drought, lack of roads and markets, a growing population pressing against the narrow limits of subsistence farming, resentment at the harsh attitude of the Governor and the Assembly which sought to continue slavery under the mask of freedom. If freedom 'is the process by which an image of the future is consciously realised' the hope the free worker cherished in 1834 had become the despair of 1865.

The Morant Bay rising confirmed the British Parliament in its view that the government of the majority of the people, all of whom were the descendants of slaves, could not be left in the hands of a minority of merchants and planters, most of whom were concerned with preserving the earlier economic and social structure. Jamaica was made a Crown Colony in 1866. As in the case of Trinidad, the British government considered it far too dangerous a step to widen the franchise. It eliminated it instead. Paternalism took the place of oligarchy, but the traditional authoritarianism remained.

The constitutional change was important. Jamaica, under the direction of the Governor, John Peter Grant, a man of exceptional ability, established the beginnings of a civil service and of the medical and educational services, and introduced sweeping improvements in the judicial service.

Larger issues were involved. The forces of social and economic change were gathering swiftly. Exactly a hundred years after the revolution of the 1830s had set the worker free, the revolution of the 1930s brought him to political power. Two sections of the West Indian population which for long had been separate, the middle-class intellectuals and the labouring people, were brought together to form one society. Cipriani, a white Trinidadian, had symbolized this coming union in the 1920s. It had been symbolized in the 1860s in the brown middle-class nationalist Robert Osborn who at first had taken the view that the salvation of the planting economy was necessary to Jamaica's salvation and who later, looking at the success of the small-holders, had said that 'that there is now more substantial wealth in the colony than twenty years ago, for whatever a man possesses is his own'.[100] It had been symbolized also in the association of two Jamaicans, brown and black, George William Gordon and Paul Bogle. It had been foretold by a Jamaican in 1839:

'I have said . . . that the African race must ultimately become dominant in the West Indies . . . it cannot be said that there is any impossibility in the European landholder continuing to cultivate his estates, and enjoy the profits of it in security, though the great majority of those filling superior positions in Jamaica should be descendants of the African race. This to be sure is the grand problem to be solved: this is the revolution which to bring about gradually and beneficially will require the exercise of great wisdom and policy; and here is the high and honourable task which is thrown upon the nation.'[101]

Two root causes of the sweeping changes that took place in the 1930s were population growth and a change in attitudes and selfconcepts within the West Indian people.

During the period of slavery deaths exceeded births. The population never replenished itself by natural increase. The effective field force was kept at strength by the annual importation of slaves. In Jamaica between the years 1817 and 1829 the slave population fell from 346,150 to 322,400. A part of this decrease was due to manumissions, but certainly not all of it. In his classic study, *The Population of Jamaica*, G. Roberts points out that with the exception of Barbados the excess of deaths over births was general throughout the slave population of the West Indies.

Emancipation opened up a new period in which this trend was reversed. Throughout the islands the population grew steadily, the rate of growth varying according to circumstances. Trinidad, during the period of heavy East Indian immigration, had an annual rate of growth ranging from 3·1 per cent to 0·9 per cent, about double that of Jamaica, whereas the rate of growth for Barbados and the Leeward Islands was by comparison low because of emigration. In the period when Trinidad was importing people these islands were exporting them. In 1871 the population of the West Indies was 513,901. By 1946 it had more than doubled itself, reaching a total of 1,011,684.

The land was carrying too many people. In some islands the density per square mile was very heavy. In 1960 it was 441 in Montserrat, 411 in St Vincent, 544 in Grenada. In Barbados it reached the extraordinary figure of 1,159 to the square mile. Since many of the islands are mountainous and much of the land not suited to cultivation the density figures should be doubled in order to get an accurate picture of the pressure of people on the land. The pressure was increased by the fact that, apart from Trinidad, all the islands were wholly dependent on agriculture.

The chief reason for the increase in population was the reduction in the death-rate through the control and prevention of those environ-mental diseases which had made the islands a graveyard for thousands of European troops and African slaves in the eighteenth century. Typhoid, typhus, malaria, dysentery, or the bloody flux, yellow fever and cholera were the killers. In 1741 the British army lost two out of every three men from fever during its attack on Cartagena. Yellow fever was the greatest ally of Toussaint in the Haitian war against the French. In 1851 cholera killed one-tenth of the population of Barbados, Jamaica and the Bahamas. After 1880 widespread improvements in the medical services and in public health resulted in a steady decline in the death-rate. More people lived, and lived longer.

After 1870 the pressure of poverty was eased by the cultivation of crops other than sugar-cane, such as sea-island cotton, cocoa and bananas. This last was of special importance in Jamaica where the crop was first grown and developed by smallholders. Cuba had already been shipping bananas to the United States when in the 1860s a few shipments were sent from the north coast ports of Jamaica to Boston. The trade expanded gradually to the point where steamers began to call for cargoes. From this time it grew swiftly. Both large and small planters turned from sugar to this new and profitable crop. But the smallholder was never displaced by bananas as the white smallholder had been displaced two centuries earlier by sugar-cane. Bananas can be grown on a wide range of cultivable land. They need no processing, and the tree produces its fruit within twelve months with comparatively little labour. In most islands there was an increase in the diversification of crops, and in the number of smallholdings. In Jamaica 'between 1881 and 1911 the class of provision planters, who may be equated with the small farmers, increased from 47,000 or one-sixth of the gainfully occupied population to 142,000 or one-third. . . . The history of the small farmer from 1865 to 1910 is therefore one of very considerable economic success.'[102]

But the hard-won security of the small farmer was itself threatened by his children. Lewis in his discussion of industrialization in the West Indies, in 1949, pointed out that the land reached the limit of its capacity to carry people some 30 or 40 years ago, that is, between 1890 and 1900. After 1900 the number engaged in agriculture tended to decline. There were many landless people who could not afford to go abroad and these moved into the cities, creating shanty towns, living from hand to mouth, the first proletariat of the West Indies. When the United States and the Central American republics closed the doors of entry by restrictive legislation in the 1920s, large numbers of workers returned home, increasing the number of those who exchanged the drab poverty of the countryside for the abject squalor and festering discontent of the towns. Unemployment was endemic by 1930. The fall of prices for export crops during the 1930s, the spread of Panama disease which almost wiped out the banana industry in Jamaica, the hopeless frustration of people shut out from participating in the government by a limited franchise and confined within narrow social limits by rigid class lines and social attitudes all bred active discontent. Those who had eyes, could see, in the early 1930s, signs of a coming storm.

The storm broke in 1938. It resulted from a combination of aspiration and frustration, of new social attitudes and old social inequalities.

New attitudes had developed among black and coloured West Indians. With the spread of primary education and the increase, though small, in the opportunities for secondary education, the middle class had grown and it included many more black persons in proportion to brown. The number of professional people in Jamaica, for example, increased from 2,000 in 1844 to 20,000 in 1943. Among them were intellectuals who, resenting colonial rule, became the advocates of a national movement.

The most important social change was that which took place in the mind of the black West Indian. It had to do with the way in which he saw himself and his role in the society of which he was a part. The change is not yet complete. The marks of two centuries of slavery are not erased easily; and they could not be erased without an increase in political power and in social status. These increases came in the period following 1938.

In 1952 a sociologist, undertaking a field study in one of the West Indian islands, records a black man as saying that 'the people here honour the higher colour more than the black. If I went to my bed and woke in the morning as a white man I would be in an entirely different position though still poor.'[103] A lower middle-class black man declared that 'white people have not treated the black people good so the black people in turn have become full of hatred for the white. It is not right that he should be but he has'.[104] A light coloured middle-class man said the trouble was that 'whiteness is the symbol of good and blackness of bad. The whiter you are the better you are; the blacker you are the worse you are'.[105] Under the system of slavery it was difficult for a black man not to accept this judgement, because this was the sentence that the economic system passed upon him and because the culture decreed for him a place of inferiority.

This acceptance by black people of the doctrine of black badness and white virtue was attacked vigorously by Marcus Garvey, a Negro who was born at St Ann's Bay in Jamaica in 1887. As a young man he travelled in Central America and in England, and was disturbed at the hardships and injustices under which he found many of his race were suffering. While in England he read *Up from Slavery*, the autobiography of a famous American Negro leader, Booker T. Washington, and he says that then his doom of being a race leader dawned upon him.[106]

Garvey returned to Jamaica, founded the Universal Negro Improvement Association, and called on all people of Negro blood to join a great crusade to promote the spirit of race pride and love.

From Jamaica Garvey went to the United States in order to win adherents to his movement. In a short time he gained a large following for he was a natural orator with a message that kindled a feeling of self-respect in the hearts of black people. He advocated setting up a great Negro kingdom in Africa, founding a Black Star Line of ships and a black order of nursing. These plans seemed grandiose at the time. With the setting-up of independent African Kingdoms they have now all become realities. Garvey's plans touched the imagina/ tion of millions of people, but many of them came to nothing. He died knowing that much of his work had collapsed. Personally honest and devoted to his cause, an orator and visionary, he was misled by some of those whom he most trusted. He also aroused opposition among a number of white and black people. In the end he was sentenced to imprisonment in the United States and later deported to Jamaica. When Jamaica became independent in 1962 the government named Marcus Garvey as one of the island's national heroes. His tomb, which stands in a Kingston park, has become a national shrine. Garvey remains an important and impressive figure in West Indian history because he liberated so many of his own race, teaching them self-respect and pride in their heritage. The long night of slavery had almost destroyed these feelings. Garvey revived them with his flaming words and his vision. Technically the Act of Emancipation had wiped out all discrimination on the ground of race, but race and colour still determined the Negro's inferior place in West Indian society. Garvey changed this.

Linked with this change was that by which West Indians came to discover their identity as people. This expressed itself in the works of a number of writers and artists who for the first time wrote of the West Indian people and portrayed the West Indian landscape. The movement flowered in the years after 1938 but it had its beginning in the troubled exciting decade when new concepts of individual worth and national identity merged with a labour movement that grew out of riots and bloodshed in Trinidad, Barbados, St Kitts and Jamaica and became the most powerful political force in the islands.

The outbreak occurred during the years from 1934 to 1938. In 1935 sugar workers in St Kitts struck for more pay. Some months later there was trouble amongst the workers in St Vincent where the St Vincent Workingman's Association was formed, to press for land settlement and for a new constitution. In Castries, the capital of St Lucia, coal heavers went on strike, but there was no violence.

There followed strikes and riots on the Trinidad oil fields where Uriah Buzz Butler emerged as the leader of thousands of workers. Arms had to be used to restore order. Shortly afterwards there was rioting in Bridgetown over the detention of Clement Payne who had gone from Trinidad to Barbados to persuade the sugar workers to unite for more wages and better conditions. In May 1938 disorders broke out in Jamaica on a sugar estate in the western parish of West, moreland. Unemployment, poverty, resentment at a social order that gave them neither security nor dignity and the innumerable griev, ances of many years exploded in strikes and riots in Kingston and in other parts of the island. What happened was not the work of agitators. It was the unplanned and disorganized action of people expressing their discontent.

Leaders emerged, some from the group of middle-class intel, lectuals, like Grantley Adams of Barbados and Norman Manley of Jamaica; others from the middle classes and from the great mass of the people, Robert Bradshaw in St Kitts, Vere Bird in Antigua, Alexander Bustamante in Jamaica. Under their leadership the labour movement, in which Cipriani and Marryshow of Grenada had been pioneers, became an effective political force.

Following on the riots of 1937 and 1938 the British government sent out a Royal Commission to the West Indies under Lord Moyne to inquire into the causes and to make recommendations with refer, ence to them; and in 1940 Parliament passed the first of the Colonial Development Acts under which money was provided for carrying out the recommendations of the Moyne Commission and for assist, ing in the development of the islands. A new philosophy prevailed in Britain, pointing to the end of Crown Colony government and to the setting of independence as a goal. The day of the limited fran, chise and of class legislation was drawing to a close; and at this critical period the labour movement provided the West Indian worker with an organization of his own through which he could make his claims on society.

8   From Colony to Country

IN 1938 THE WEST INDIES moved out of the nineteenth into the twentieth century.

The first indication of this was the development of a labour movement. It was still true in the West Indies of the 1930s that though slavery had been abolished and nine out of ten people in the population set free, there had been little change in the old pattern of exploitation. The social and economic structure remained that of a small group of white persons controlling the major portion of property holding the key posts in government and industry and possessing political control. The restricted franchise revealed the situation. In 1934 in Trinidad, then a Crown Colony, there were 25,000 people who had the vote out of a total population of 400,000. Barbados in 1937 had 5,000 voters in a population of 200,000. Beneath the narrow uppermost tier of the ruling class of whites was a broader tier of the middle class, made up of technicians, professional and subprofessional people, tradesmen, merchants, civil servants, the majority of them brown. The lowest supporting tier was the great mass of the population, mostly black. In Trinidad the middle and the lowest tiers included East Indians as well as Negroes.

The year 1938 showed that the road to equality of opportunity for the mass of people was through active protest. The price of protest was 47 killed, more than 400 injured, and over 1,000 arrests. Out of the protest emerged an organized labour movement.

There had been earlier groupings and associations of the working classes. In the towns, men and women of limited means had organized their own social security through Burial Scheme Societies, Friendly Societies and Benevolent Societies and Lodges. These,

82

supported by weekly contributions, assisted members with grants to pay for medical expenses in time of illness and to meet the cost of a decent burial. Agricultural societies and associations of primary school teachers acted as pressure groups, putting in claims for roads, hospitals, markets, water supplies and the like. They were a training ground for the politically inclined, giving the opportunity for leadership in pressing the claims of rural communities.

Occasionally an exceptional leader formed a small union, such as the Carpenters, Bricklayers and Painters Union in Jamaica in 1907, the Jamaica Trades and Labour Union of 1907 and the Trinidad Working Mens' Association of the 1890s. These had little power. After the First World War attempts were made to form other unions and to revive old ones, the most notable being the Working Men's Association in Trinidad. While the law permitted the formation of Unions its provisions discouraged union action. The Jamaica Trade Union Law of 1919 did not allow peaceful picketing and it did not release the Unions from liability for suits for damages as a result of strikes. The Moyne Report of 1939 pointed out that only in Guyana were trade unions protected against these damages, and it went on to say that in Jamaica the provision had been expressly omitted from the law of 1919 at the instance of the government of the colony.

In the three years from 1938 to 1941 more labour legislation was passed in the islands than in the preceding century. It embodied a labour code, and this was a marked advance for the Orde Brown Report on labour conditions in the West Indies had pointed out that up to 1938 there was practically no provision for regulating industrial relations, and no effective labour legislation. The Royal Commission of 1939 recommended the establishment of Labour Departments, and the appointment of a Labour Adviser to the West Indian governments.

The need for an organized labour movement was clear, for the worker had been neglected for generations. At the Conference in Dominica in 1932 some West Indian leaders, among them Rawle of Dominica, had pointed to the squalid hovels in which the labouring classes lived and had deplored the failure of Crown Colony govern- ment to improve these conditions. The Moyne Commission's Report, written during the war but not published in full until 1945, declared that the Imperial and Colonial governments had failed to make radical reforms and called for modern labour legislation. Legislation, however, has little effect without leadership, and fortunately leaders of exceptional quality were forthcoming in 1938. In some cases the leadership was charismatic in character. This was so in Trinidad, where Uriah Buzz Butler succeeded in building up a massive following among the people; but although he consistently advocated self-government for Trinidad and Tobago he proved 'inadequate to the task either of forming a political party or of organizing the oil-field workers'.[107]

In Jamaica two leaders emerged. One was Alexander Bustamante, whose Bustamante Industrial Trade Union had, in 1948, a membership of 46,538 out of an organized labour force of 57,000. Bustamante was born on 24 February 1884 in the parish of Hanover. He was the son of an Irish planter named Robert Constantine Clark and his wife Mary Wilson. It is reported that at the age of 15 he was adopted by a Spanish sea-captain and taken to Spain, that he joined the Spanish army and served in Casa Blanca and Morocco, and that while in Spain he took the name of his benefactor, Bustamante. Up to 1944 his name was Alexander Clark Bustamante, but in that year, by deed pool, he changed it to William Alexander Bustamante. After travelling extensively in Cuba, the United States and Central America he returned to Jamaica in 1932, immediately began to take a part in local affairs, and in 1938 by force of personality and political skill became the island's labour leader:

'Flamboyant, unpredictable, indefatigable, the tall energetic Jamaican drew crowds in the thousands and was the bane of the police as his listeners blocked streets and side-walks. . . . There was never any doubt of where he stood. He was for the working man . . . to the point of sedition, and the workers were equally for him:

> We will follow Bustamante
> We will follow Bustamante
> Till we die. . . .'[108]

84

The other leader was Norman Washington Manley, Q.C., veteran of the First World War, holder of the military medal and founder of the People's National Party. Manley, who was born in the parish of Manchester on 4 July 1893, was the son of a dealer in produce. After a brilliant scholastic record at Jamaica College, where he created a record for the 100 yards dash that stood alone until it was equalled by his son in 1958, he was awarded the Rhodes Scholarship in 1914 and entered Jesus College, Oxford. On the outbreak of war he joined the Royal Field Artillery. After demobilization he returned to law and completed his legal training in 1921, gaining a Certificate of Honour and becoming Lee Prizeman of Gray's Inn. He returned to Jamaica in 1922 and soon became the islands' outstanding lawyer.

Manley and Bustamante worked together closely in the months following the 1938 riots, and after Bustamante was interned Manley ran the Bustamante Industrial Trade Union, building up the membership and negotiating the first all-island sugar agreement between the union and the Sugar Manufacturers Association. After Bustamante was released from prison he broke with Manley, the two leaders becoming rivals for power, with Bustamante as leader of the Jamaica Labour Party and the Bustamante Industrial Trade Union, and Manley as leader of the People's National Party.

In Barbados another Oxford-trained lawyer, Grantley Adams, emerged as labour leader. After returning from Oxford he had been an outspoken critic of the privileges and powers of the planters. In 1938 he successfully defended Clement Payne who had gone to Barbados from Trinidad to organize the sugar workers, and who was prosecuted by the Police. Adams soon became the undisputed leader of the Barbados Labour Party and the Barbados Labour Union.

In St Kitts-Nevis where almost all the good land was owned by the estates and working class conditions were deplorably bad, a newly formed Trade Union under Robert Bradshaw won a struggle for better wages and then swept into power as the Workers League. Vere Bird in Antigua had similar success, supporting the worker and at the same time organizing his union so that it also won the elections. In all the West Indian islands trade unions were successfully organized and in most cases they won control of the local legislature.

The labour movement had political as well as economic objectives. The demand was not only for higher wages and better living conditions but also for drastic changes in the constitution so as to take power out of the hand of the propertied classes and put it in the hand of the people. The results of government on a restricted franchise were clear for all to see, and the leaders of the labour movement concluded that the social reforms they demanded would be obtained only by gaining control of the government. They demanded universal adult suffrage, elected legislatures and executive councils responsible to the legislatures.

The Moyne Commission had noted this. It reported that many West Indians were convinced that social reconstruction depended for their initiation and administration on greater participation by the people in the business of government, but the Moyne proposals for constitutional reform were out of date almost before they were published.

The first constitutional change was in Jamaica, where a new constitution, introduced in 1944, provided for universal adult suffrage and a bicameral legislature in which power rested with a wholly elected House of Representatives. Nominated members were relegated to a Legislative Council, which had delaying powers only. In 1950 Trinidad and Tobago was granted a new constitution with a unicameral legislature in which there was an elected majority. By 1951 Grenada, St Vincent, St Lucia, Dominica, Antigua, St Kitts-Nevis and Montserrat all had this type of representative government. Further reforms were introduced in Trinidad and Tobago, so that by 1960 there were no nominated members in its Legislative Council.

The extension of the franchise changed the social and political structure radically. It occurred at the beginning of a period of intense economic activity and of a drive for industrialization, and the political and economic changes combined to break down many of the race and colour barriers to various occupations and to social position. The rigid three-tier caste structure gave way to a class structure in which there was increasing vertical mobility.

West Indian leaders also sought to make the executive council responsible to the representative legislatures and not to the Crown. By 1960 most of the islands had achieved this, and had full responsibility for the management of their internal affairs.

There are close links between West Indian political parties and the trade unions. The roots of power are in the trade unions. Phelps, in a study of the labour movement in Jamaica, pointed out that the period of world change between 1937 and 1945, covering the last half of a world-wide depression and the most disastrous of wars was trade unionism's greatest period of incubation and that in the 20 years between 1937 and 1957 the West Indian labour movement, starting from almost zero, gained a larger proportion of the wage-earning population as members than had the trade unions of the United States.

In the year of the riots in Trinidad there was a young Trinidadian scholar at Oxford called Eric Williams. He graduated with First Class Honours of that University in 1935, and in 1938 was completing his work for the degree of Doctor of Philosophy. In his own words he was for seven years a part, however small, of noble and inspiring traditions, attracted most of all by the 'Oxford of Scholarship, the Oxford of the Reformation, the Civil War and the British Empire'. The result of his work was *Capitalism and Slavery*, the book on which his reputation as a historian chiefly rests; and a book that was one of the first, along with the *Black Jacobins* of C. L. R. James, in presenting the history of the Caribbean from the point of view of a scholar of the Caribbean.

After teaching history at Howard University where he was Professor of Political and Social Science, Dr Williams worked for a time with the Caribbean Commission, and then entered politics in his native land, founding the People's National Movement in 1956. He became the first Chief Minister of Trinidad and Tobago, and in 1962 achieved the honour of being his country's first Prime Minister.

Dr Williams' achievement in organizing and maintaining a political party in Trinidad is notable, important socially as well as politically, for Trinidad is the newest of the West Indian communities, the most cosmopolitan, the least homogeneous. Like Guyana it has two large racial groups, the Negro and East Indian. It differs from the other English-speaking islands in its development as a sugar plantation island through East Indian indentured workers, and in having no tradition of colonial representative government. The achievement of Dr Williams in building a national movement that cuts across race and religion is remarkable.

The goals of West Indian leadership in the 1940s were self-government for each island as a step towards independence, and better standards of living through economic development. At first an attempt was made to gain independence through federation. Labour leaders, like Cipriani of Trinidad, Marryshow of Grenada and Thorne of Guiana had advocated federation and independence, and in 1944 a West Indies Labour Conference unanimously approved a resolution in favour of Federation.[109] In the following year the Secretary of the State for the Colonies instructed the governors of the West Indian colonies to put the issue of Federation before the legislatures for debate. Two years later, in 1947, a Conference of West Indian leaders in Montego Bay accepted 'the principle of a Federation in which each constituent unit retains complete control over all matters except those specifically assigned to the Federal Government'.[110] The Conference set up a Standing Closer Association Committee made up of 17 representatives from the various colonial legislatures to formulate constitutional proposals. The Standing Closer Association Committee produced its report in 1949. At this point Guyana, British Honduras and the British Virgin Islands fell out. There were danger signs in the voting in other legislatures. In Trinidad the proposals were accepted but only two out of nine elected members voted for them, so that the decision was made by the colonial government and not by the representatives of the people. The Barbados and Jamaica Legislatures accepted the proposals as a basis for discussion only.

Discussions on federation continued up to 1957, when the West Indian and the United Kingdom governments agreed to establish a Federal government of the West Indies. A Standing Federation Committee was set up to prepare the terms, the outcome being proposals for an extremely weak central government with an annual budget of £2 million and without the power to raise revenue by taxation. There was no national stamp, no common coinage, nor was there agreement on the free movement of people within the federal boundaries. The arrangements reflected 'the triumph of the sentiments of insularity over those of nationalism'.[111] The Federal government was established in January 1958. It was dissolved in 1962, the year in which the Federation was to have become independent.

One of the immediate causes for the collapse of the Federation arose out of the political rivalry between Manley and Bustamante. Manley, at that time Premier, decided to put to Jamaica through a referendum the question whether the island should remain in the federation or seek independence by itself. The referendum was held on 19 September 1961. Only 61 per cent of the Jamaican electorate voted. Of these 54·11 per cent rallied to Bustamante's slogan: 'Independence – Yes, Federation – No.' The voting followed Jamaican party lines. Among the mass of the people there was little understanding of the issues at stake.

After the result of the Jamaican referendum was known, there was hope for an Eastern Caribbean Union based on Trinidad, with a central government that had greater powers. This depended on the attitude of Trinidad, which had more than half the population of the eastern islands and more than half the resources. Was salvage possible? Not after the decision of Trinidad and Tobago to withdraw. The issue was not put to the electorate in the Trinidad General Election in the autumn of the year, but the comments of Dr Williams on the 'tom-foolery of federation' and his frequently expressed opposition to any kind of federation other than one with a strong centre gave little ground for hope. After the Trinidad election in December 1961 the General Council of the People's National Movement approved a resolution that Trinidad and Tobago should reject participation in any Eastern Caribbean Conference and proceed forthwith to independence. It stated in uncompromising terms that the unitary state of Trinidad and Tobago would be willing to consider incorporation within it of any island in the area whose people wished for this. The remaining eight islands, the 'Little Eight', proceeded to discuss proposals for a federation; but there is little likelihood of this being established.

But the real causes went deep. They are part of the Caribbean tradition of separatism and colonial fragmentation. The debates at the Montego Bay Conference and in the island legislatures as well as at the London Conference of 1956 showed that there was no strong West Indian national sentiment. To make use of the title of a West Indian novel, *An island is a world*:[112] 'For West Indians, the island is, in most contexts, the most compelling area symbol. A man who says "I am a Jamaican" or "I am a Barbadian" is very likely expressing the broadest allegiance he knows.'[113] This results from the sharing up of the islands by a number of distant powers, and the attachment of the islands as separate units to the metropolitan administration. The unfortunate decision of the government of the United Kingdom to defederate the Leeward Islands into two or three small units strengthened the fissiparous tendencies within the region.

Another difficulty lay in the fact that Jamaica, with half the population and half the land area of the Federation was 1,200 miles from the Federal capital in Port-of-Spain. The island had 'little or no connection with and less fellow feeling for the people of the Eastern Caribbean, who are themselves divided by geography, history and strong local attachments'.[114]

Also, the disproportion between two of the units in the Federation and the other eight was extreme. Jamaica and Trinidad had 83 per cent of the total land area of the Federation, 77 per cent of its population and three-quarters of its wealth. In both these territories the Opposition party in the Federal government won majorities, so that most of the cabinet seats went to the small territories where the Federal party had majorities.

The imbalance between the two large units and the remaining eight was made greater by the pace of economic development in Jamaica and Trinidad. These two islands made remarkable progress in developing new industries, and every step forward widened the gap between themselves and the Eight. The spur to economic development was population growth. Both islands were extremely sensititive about any attempt to lessen their own power to direct this

drive, and about any attempt to add to their already formidable problems. Jamaica, under pressure from its unemployed, was apprehensive
about having to give aid to the small islands. Trinidad, short of job
opportunities for its own people, rejected freedom of movement since
this would have meant finding more jobs in the island for more
people. The difficulty was increased because the leaders of the two
large units refused to go to the centre. They knew where power was,
and they stayed with it. Besides they had little confidence in the
leadership of the Federal government.

For its part the Federal government was so weak that it could do
little even for the small islands. Its first task was to win the support
and backing of the two large units. This it failed to do, and was
thereby doomed. Its position was made more difficult by the
behaviour of the United Kingdom government.

Britain had welcomed the proposal for a Federation of the West
Indies because she was engaged in bringing her colonies to independence as quickly as possible.

'The self image of the British Colonial Office is clearly that of what
might be called imperial fission into a family of nations ... and one
gets the impression that the Colonial Office is very busy trying to
push all its little birds out of the window and forcing them to fly
by themselves.'[115]

The two large units suspected the Colonial Office of trying to pass
on its economic burdens to them, while the smaller islands did not
wish to exchange dependence on London for dependence on Port-
of-Spain or Kingston. They knew that John Bull was less prosperous
than in former times but they were certain 'there is a lot of milk left in
the old Bull yet'.[116] Suspicions were strengthened by the fact that
Britain gave no firm offer of additional assistance over a period in the
interests of her small colonies. Resentment was added to suspicion
when in 1961 the Imperial Parliament passed a Commonwealth
Immigrants Act to control immigration from Commonwealth
countries. Trinidad was especially concerned since the closing of
United Kingdom doors was bound to intensify pressure for freedom

of movement with the Federation. Following on this came Britain's decision to seek admission to the European Common Market. West Indians, whose bananas and sugar survive because of Common/wealth preference agreements, knew that they would be bankrupt if special terms of entry for their products could not be arranged.

In August 1962 Jamaica and Trinidad and Tobago became inde/pendent countries. The constitution of each of these two nations shows the influence of the English Parliamentary system and indicates the value placed by the nation on equality. In each of these instances the draft constitution was widely discussed. There was no sharp departure from the pattern of the United Kingdom, either in prac/tice or in philosophy, as there was in the United States in 1784. The constitutional ties with the British Crown and the Commonwealth were retained. The Sovereign of England is the Sovereign of each country, and as such is the nominal head of the Executive. Parlia/ment consists of the Sovereign, a nominated Senate and a House of Representatives elected by adult suffrage. The members of the elected House are termed Members of Parliament. The Sovereign is repre/sented by a Governor/General appointed on the advice of the Prime Minister. The leader of the majority party in the House of Repre/sentatives is appointed Prime Minister by the Governor/General. Under the constitution the Prime Minister selects his ministers. The Prime Minister and Ministers form a Cabinet that is collectively responsible to Parliament.

It is possibly a unique feature of Jamaica's Constitution that it confers certain functions on the Leader of the Opposition, and in this way seeks to reinforce the two/party system. Other constitutions recognize a 'Leader of the Opposition' but the Jamaica Constitution, in an effort to avoid dictatorship and one/party rule, gives certain specific functions to the Leader of the Opposition. Some appoint/ments to high office are made by the Governor/General on the advice of the Prime Minister. The Chief Justice is appointed in this way; so also are the President of the Court of Appeal and certain members of the three Commissions that are responsible for the subordinate courts, the civil service and the police. In making these appointments the

Jamaica Constitution requires that the Leader of the Opposition should be consulted, and he has the right to express his views to the Prime Minister and the Governor-General. In selecting members of the Senate the Governor-General is required to appoint approximately one-third on the advice of the Leader of the Opposition and the rest on the advice of the Prime Minister.

This attempt to entrench a two-party system in the constitution is the direct opposite of the line taken by some African states, which advocate the one-party system as being more in line with African tradition. One reason for this attempt lies in the fact that the two-party system is very new. It developed after 1944. Also, since a country with a tradition of authoritarianism does not easily tolerate opposition, it was important to protect the right to oppose. Furthermore there is no doubt that the possibility of an alternative government aids in securing good government.

The constitutions of Trinidad and Tobago and of Jamaica provide full safeguards for rights considered essential in a democracy, such as the regular calling of Parliament and free elections at stated intervals.

In Trinidad there was some advocacy of proportional representation on the basis of racial groupings, but this was generally rejected. Public opinion took the view that this would have meant entrenching racial differences in the constitution of the country.

The other territories in the Caribbean and on the American mainland are well on the road to independence. British Guiana became the independent state of Guyana in May 1966. British Honduras will become independent Belice in due time.

Colonialism has become a word of abuse, and a colony a badge of shame. Yet West Indians recognize that they gained substantial benefits from their long association with Britain. Each island is served by a civil service organized and trained on the pattern of the British civil service. At first all senior posts were held by persons from the United Kingdom, and all the lower posts by local people, but West Indians gradually extended their influence and power to the point where they now hold the chief posts. In each island the police force has a long honourable tradition of efficient service. The administration of justice is maintained by lawyers trained in the British tradition, with a profound respect for justice and the rule of law.

In exercising policy and putting legislation into effect the govern- ments in all the islands make use of local government institutions and of a number of statutory boards created to carry out special tasks. Industrial and Agricultural Development Corporations, School Boards, Public Service Commissions, and scores of voluntary and semi-government organizations indicate an active concern among the West Indian people with their own affairs. There are professional organizations such as Teachers Associations, branches of the British Medical Association and Law Societies.

The production and export of the main crops of the islands are managed by Commodity Associations many of which are regional in character. Prominent among these are the West Indies Sugar Manufacturers Association, one of the most efficient and highly organized groups in the West Indies, which undertakes among its other duties the task of international bargaining and negotiation; the West Indies Citrus Growers Association, the Jamaica Banana Producers and the Windward Islands Banana Growers Associa- tion. Each island has its Boy Scouts, Girl Guides and Rovers; and there are active branches of the Commonwealth Chambers of Com- merce of the Caribbean as well as of Rotary, the Kiwanis, the Lions, the Red Cross and the Order of St John. The standards of profes- sional practice and ethics are jealously safeguarded.

In the independent West Indian countries steps have been taken to create the organizations that are essential for nationhood, such as a national banking system, the control of employment in the interests of citizens, and adequate representation overseas through High Com- missioners. Jamaica and Trinidad and Tobago have High Com- missioners and Ambassadors to the United Nations, Canada, and the United Kingdom, as well as to other nations with whom the West Indies have close relationships.

West Indian leaders have expressed frequently their debt to Britain for their political institutions and for a tradition of public service. Their chief problems are not political but economic. There are no bitter racial minorities, no tribal rivalries, no social traditions nor systems of organization that run counter to Western parliamentary democracy. But West Indians know that they have no security. They watched with dismay the growth of racial hatred between Africans and East Indians in Guyana. They know that a tribalism of colour can develop quickly, as it has done in South Africa. Antigua has beaches and a sparkling sea, St Kitts an attractive climate and fertile soil, Grenada, St Lucia, St Vincent and Dominica great natural beauty and good land for bananas and sugar-cane, but they in common with Barbados, Jamaica and Trinidad and Tobago are engaged in a search for security. Their survival depends on the development of a new concept of international aid by which money for development can be obtained without economic aid being used as an instrument for the foreign policy of larger, more powerful countries. There is growing bitterness among West Indians at the fact that an interdependent world, in which there is no such thing as an economically independent country, lays down for them the same criteria for economic development as for large nations.

The West Indian search for security is a twofold one; for the means to pay one's way through economic development and for a national unity that comprehends race and colour.

9   Search for Security

THE BASIC PROBLEM of the islands is that of population pressure; of a rising tide of people beating insistently against limited land
resources.[117] The total population of the West Indies is $3\frac{1}{2}$ million
people. This is not a large figure, but the islands are small. Cuba has
twice as many people with five times as much land. The Dominican
Republic has as large a population with $3\frac{1}{2}$ times as much land. On
the mainland, in Central America, the only country with a larger
population is Mexico. Guatamala has the same number of people
with five times as much land. The smallest of the republics, El Salva-
dor, is the size of the West Indies but its population is smaller by a
million. In Europe the Republic of Ireland is three times as large as
the West Indies and its population is half a million smaller. Wales
has an area of 8,000 square mlies, the same as that of the West Indies,
with a population of $2\frac{1}{2}$ millions.

Even Trinidad, which went in search of immigrants in 1850, now
faces the problem of too rapid population growth. Over the last
hundred years the high rate of natural increase of a quarter of a million indentured East Indian labourers, and of immigrants from Barbados, Grenada and other neighbouring islands, has transformed the
island's population. In 1871 the Trinidad census showed a population of 126,700 persons; in 1965 it was about 900,000, over four
times as many. In each decade the number of people in the island
grew by at least 10 per cent, reaching a point where a Calypso singer
voiced the general feeling over the invasion of Trinidad by indigent
small island people:

Small island, go back where you belong.
You come from Grenada in a fishing boat,
And now you're wearing a saga-boy coat,
Small island, go back where you belong. . . .

In the Eastern Caribbean, people moved to those lands that were short of labour. Islands wholly given up to sugar, like Barbados, Antigua and St Kitts, lost people during this period. Between 1863 and 1870 about 16,000 Barbadians emigrated to British and Dutch Guiana, St Croix and Trinidad, and by 1901 seven out of every hundred people in Trinidad were Barbadians. After this date the main flow from Barbados was to the United States and Panama.

Jamaicans migrated to the mainland, not the Eastern Caribbean. In 1881 the Governor reported that workers were leaving the island at the rate of 1,000 a month for Panama and some of the Central American republics, many going to Panama to work with the French Company that was attempting to dig the Panama Canal. Emigration to the Isthmus died away with the failure of the French, but grew to large proportions when the Americans began work on the canal in 1904. The total number of Jamaican emigrants to Panama between 1881 and 1911 was 43,000. After 1911 New York, the northern industrial cities of the United States and the cane fields of Cuba absorbed 77,000 Jamaican workers.

Roberts[118] has pointed to the beneficial effects of this early migra-tion, which supplied Trinidad, the Guianas and the Dutch islands of Curacao and Aruba with the labour supply that they needed, and which put a temporary check to population increase in Barbados, where the population stood at 182,900 in 1891 and declined to 156,000 in 1921. Without migration the Barbados population would have reached 410,000 by 1946, with an intolerable burden of 2,500 to the square mile. Barbados and Jamaica also benefited from the remittances that migrants sent back. This amounted to £821,000 between 1911 and 1920. After 1921 emigration fell off because the United States and many of the Latin American countries passed laws restricting immigration. The traditional escape hatches on the mainland were closed, and population pressure in the islands mounted.

West Indians went overseas in order to find better work and greater opportunities for self-advancement. For by 1900 the islands, with the exception of Trinidad, were overpopulated. The intensity of the pressure on the land can be judged from the figures for Jamaica, where approximately one-half of the total land area is not cultivable. Jamaica has only one-seventh of its area in flat lands, and only about one-eighth under cultivation, when permanent grass is included. On this basis it could carry at European peasant standards a density of 60 per square mile, but its present density is 364. Arthur Lewis has pointed out that the process has gone as far as it can, and that the land reached the limit of its capacity to carry people some 30 or 40 years ago.[119]

The fall in the death-rate has contributed to the rate of population growth, especially since the 1920s. Over the period from 1881 to 1921 the average death-rate and rate of infant mortality remained comparatively high. They declined after that year, because of extensive improvements in medical care and the growing control over environmental diseases. In Jamaica, between 1921 and 1925, the death-rate was 23·5 per thousand. For the five-year period 1946–50 the rate was only 12·9.[120] The trend was the same in all the islands. But alongside death-control there was no birth-control. At the present rate of increase the islands will double their populations in the next 25 to 30 years.

By 1950 the population pressure in most territories had become acute. Searching desperately for exits, the West Indian worker discovered England. Two centuries earlier his island had beckoned Englishmen to adventure and fortune. Now the movement was in reverse. The black colonial moved to the white mother-country, working on the underground and on the railways, in factories and mills, delivering letters, driving buses, working hard at unfamiliar jobs in a strange land in order to make life more secure for himself and his dependents. By 1965 there were over 150,000 coloured West Indian migrants in Britain, a small proportion of the total population, but one that was immediately visible.[121] In many respects the general background of West Indian migration to Britain was like the migration of Puerto Ricans to the United States in the post-war years, an effort to escape from poverty, unemployment, and severely limited social opportunity. A West Indian novelist,[122] a descendant of East Indian immigrants, described them as they gathered on an English railway platform: a man with a Nat King Cole hairstyle, a baby sucking a rubber nipple in its drooping dripping mouth, a tall ill-made Negro wearing pants of disproportionate length. The eye that saw the incongruities was closed to the fact that each plane-load, each ship-load of these immigrants, had its full measure of courage and human aspiration.

The door was closed in 1965 when the British Parliament passed a law restricting severely the number of immigrants from Common-wealth countries.

The islands all depend to an extraordinary extent on external markets. The political independence of Jamaica and Trinidad and Tobago has not changed the fact that both these countries, like Bar-bados and the Windward and Leeward Islands, have export economies, based on the exchange of a limited range of primary pro-ducts for a wide variety of foodstuffs and other consumption goods. Although each island has its special crop: Grenada nutmegs, St Vincent arrowroot, Antigua sea-island cotton, Trinidad cacao, Jamaica pimento, ginger and tobacco, the main crops are sugar and bananas, and the effects of a fall in sugar or banana prices are felt everywhere in the islands.

The trading position is made difficult by the fact that the external markets depend on the policies and practices of foreign governments. The islands are small and they produce crops at comparatively high costs, so they are at a disadvantage in competing with other producers, and they are especially vulnerable to the trading policies of the United States, Canada, and Britain.

These three countries are the traditional markets for West Indian products and West Indian governments are extremely sensitive to any action by them that appears in however remote a way to threaten the trading position of the islands. They have good reason for this. When the American War of Independence cut the West Indian lifeline of trade with North America, 15,000 slaves perished in Barbados. When Britain in the 1840s removed the duties that had protected West Indian sugar, the economy of Jamaica collapsed, producing deep social and political unrest. The situation was relieved between the years 1870 and 1900, because sugar producers in Trinidad, British Guiana, Barbados and Jamaica found a market in the United States, where a tariff wall had been set up against European beet sugar. The purpose was to protect American sugar producers, but the tariff had the effect of giving a protected market to West Indian sugar. At the end of the Spanish-American War the government of the United States, extending its economic and political power in Cuba and Puerto Rico, gave preference to sugar from these two islands. The effect was to shut out West Indian sugar, which could not compete with Cuba. In search for a market West Indian sugar producers then turned to Canada. The figures for West Indian trade in 1880 show that the United States was then the largest buyer of products from the West Indies, British Guiana and British Honduras taking 42 per cent of their exports whereas the United Kingdom took 38 per cent and Canada only 3 per cent.[123]

Canadian influence in the Caribbean became important in this century. In 1912, 1920 and 1926 Canada made trade agreements with the West Indies which gave a certain measure of preference to some West Indian products, notably sugar. Between 1890 and 1902 Canadian banks moved into the Caribbean, and later Canadian Life Insurance Companies spread throughout the English-speaking Caribbean. The establishment of a shipping service aided the increase of Canadian trade. In 1890 the Canadian government adopted the policy of subsidizing shipping services between Canada and the West Indies. It went beyond this in 1919 when it initiated a regular freight service to the Caribbean. Following on the trade agreement of 1926, regular passenger and freight services were provided through the 'Lady Boats'. The war interrupted this service. Some of the ships were lost, others needed replacing. Also, though the service was popular it was not profitable. The Lady Boats were withdrawn. Other shipping lines such as the Saguenay Terminals, now link Canada with the West Indies. The extension of Canadian influence through these various facilities and services resulted in Canada becoming an important market for West Indian products.

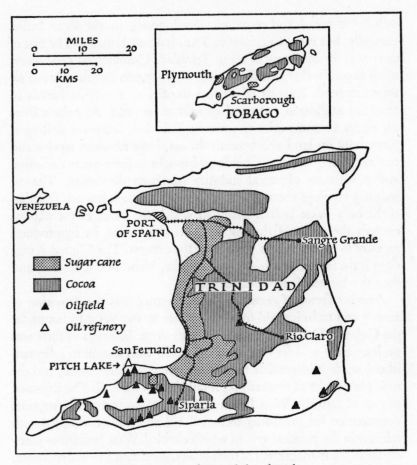

Economic map of Trinidad and Tobago

In the 1930s the United Kingdom changed its trade policy with the West Indies by giving preference to West Indian sugar, and putting import duties on a number of foreign agricultural products such as coffee, honey and citrus. The figures for 1938 show the overall result. In that year the United Kingdom took 28 per cent of West Indian exports, Canada 26 per cent and the United States only 8 per cent.

Between 1900 and 1960 important new factors profoundly

influenced social and economic development in the West Indies generally, but more especially in Trinidad and Jamaica. The first of these was the discovery of oil in Trinidad. Commercial production of oil began in that island in 1909, when 57,000 barrels of crude oil were exported. Exports of oil rose steadily to 2 million barrels in 1920, 22 million in 1940 and 46 million in 1960. At present there are about 12 companies at work in Trinidad. Intensive drilling is carried out on land and beneath the sea, large refineries receive and process great quantities of crude oil brought in from many countries, and a vigorous chemical industry has been developed. The oil industry employs about 18,000 persons. Because it has oil Trinidad is the only West Indian island in which the value of the exports exceeds the value of the imports. Petroleum and its by-products amount to more than 80 per cent of the exports. The United Kingdom is the largest purchaser and supplier, Venezuela is second, and then the United States and Canada.

Another factor of considerable importance was the provision of money and technical aid for development in the West Indies under the Colonial Development and Welfare Acts. In England there was no longer the will for empire. Two world wars fought to safeguard liberty made it impossible to continue imperial domination, and the new philosophy of trusteeship prevailed in Whitehall. The injection of capital into the West Indies and the establishment of a regional organization for providing technical aid and advice, coupled with reforms in the political system which enabled West Indians to participate in the management of their affairs, generated a new dynamism. Most of the islands accepted aid in the form of grants and advice, and the concept of planning for economic development in regional terms was soon adopted by West Indian political leaders, so that they were caught up in the exhilarating task of planning and of providing. For the first time they were in a position to find ways of diversifying their economy, establishing their priorities, and taking responsibility for their decisions. The political changes of the 1940s transformed the West Indian colonies into countries while the availability of capital and expert advice through the Development and Welfare Acts played an indispensable part in creating a new society.

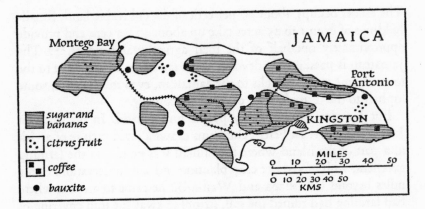

Economic map of Jamaica

While these things were taking place it was found that Jamaica had large deposits of bauxite. Two-thirds of the island is covered by a blanket of tertiary limestone, over which lies a bedspread of bauxite. In some parts deposits are thin, but there are basins and rolling pastureland where the deposits are rich. Six tons of Jamaica bauxite are needed to make a ton of aluminium as against 4 tons of Guyana bauxite, but the Jamaica reserves are very large, amounting to more than 500 million tons; they lie on or near the surface and so are mined easily; and the island lies within a thousand miles of United States ports, whereas Guyana bauxite has to be taken from Mackenzie in the interior by shallow-draft steamers to Trinidad and transhipped there, 1,200 miles southeast of Jamaica, on to ocean freighters.

Up to 1950 Jamaica had been completely dependent on agriculture. Her size, and the range of climate provided by her mountains made possible a much greater diversification of agriculture than in the other islands. She had two systems of agriculture, combining the sugar plantation economy of Barbados or St Kitts with the peasant holdings of Nevis and Montserrat. About two out of every three people in the island live on farms, and one-half of the gainfully occupied population of 615,000 is engaged in agricultural work. One-fifth of the total population, or one-third of the population over 14 years of age, finds some form of employment through agriculture.

103

The estates occupy about 60 per cent of the cultivable land. Small-holdings of from 1 to 25 acres take up about 40 per cent and provide approximately one-half of the total agricultural product.[123] The Jamaican is passionately devoted to the land, the Trinidadian to the town. Some manure sticks to the Jamaican, even in the town; some asphalt to the Trinidadian, even in the country.

But Jamaica has too many people on the land. In his study of Jamaica the novelist Peter Abrahams draws a vivid picture of a visit to a part of the island where the rainfall was good and the farming excellent, with mixed tree crop planting and soil conservation. Some miles beyond Christiana and Wait-a-Bit he came to an area where bad farming had ruined the soil, stripping away the thin covering of earth and laying bare the limestone. As they drove along, his friend, a Jamaican farmer, turned to him and said:

'"The thing is, where the land is poor the people are poor too; their spirits are poor too. You can judge the people by the state of the land. If it is healthy they are happy and healthy." He gripped the steering wheel, searching for words. "But if it is sick and dying, they are sick and dying. You understand man?"

'I understood. The Africans say "Land is the life of a people".'[124]

Bauxite, some of it in difficult inhospitable country and much of it in pleasant upland regions, gave a new strong support to Jamaica's economy. In 1956 the industry contributed £350,000 to the island's revenue. In 1961 Jamaica got £3,700,000 in royalties and taxes from bauxite. In 1952, about 400,000 tons were mined, and 1961 some 6,663,000 tons. By 1964 the industry contributed £24·1 million to the island's revenue, the exports in alumina and bauxite being valued at £33·8 million. During the period 1950 to 1960 the national income increased from £66 million to £189 million, and to this increase bauxite made a substantial contribution.

Enough has been said to show that the West Indies are not poor in the way in which many Asian and African countries are poor. The present standard of living is comparable with that of countries in the middle bracket. The trouble is that the islands are extremely vulnerable. The struggle is for economic security. Because they recognize how exposed they are West Indian governments are preoccupied with economic development. Many of them have set up Industrial Development Corporations to stimulate industrial development, and Jamaica has also an Agricultural Development Corporation to encourage investment in farming and stimulate agricultural production.

The West Indian version of Puerto Rico's 'Operation Bootstrap' has produced remarkable results. Incentive legislation aided by sterling inconvertibility during the 1940s and 1950s, and the expansion of the oil industry in Trinidad and of bauxite in Jamaica induced United States and Canadian interests to establish bases in the two larger islands. In Jamaica there are more than 100 manufacturing enterprises that have been established under the industrial incentives law, and approximately 1,000 factories enjoy the benefit of tax concessions. This activity combined with bauxite and an expanding tourist industry lifted the island's gross domestic product at factor cost from £198·2 million in 1959 to £254 million in 1963, that is, by 28·2 per cent. In terms of 1960 prices this increase amounted to 15 per cent. In Trinidad and Tobago the oil and chemical industries embarked on substantial new enterprises, one of the most important being a single-line ammonia plant, the largest of its kind in the world. The island's Industrial Development Corporation reported that between 1959 and the beginning of 1964 the island already had 143 pioneer industries already built or in the planning and construction stage, representing an investment of more than £50 million.[125]

Barbados intensified its efforts at industrialization through 'Operation Beehive', offering special incentives, including a low-cost adaptable labour force, a ten-year tax holiday, free entry of construction materials and capital equipment, full repatriation of foreign investment capital and dividends, a modern industrial estate and an efficiently run deep water harbour which has strengthened Barbados traditional position as a trading and shipping centre.

Situated as they are, the islands seek in their tourist industry to get the best of both worlds. The best known resorts are Jamaica, Barbados, Antigua and Tobago, but each island has its special attractions, crescent-shaped bays of gleaming white sand and sparkling water, an agreeable climate throughout the year, and its full share of that magic of the Antilles that first cast its spell over Columbus. The industry vitalizes the island economy. The total number of tourists visiting Jamaica in 1964 was 227,000, a 12½ per cent increase over 1963, and the estimated total expenditure by visitors was £15·6 million.[126] In Antigua the tourist trade lifted the island out of United Kingdom treasury control. The island was, in the 1940s and 1950s, poor and backward. It depended wholly on two crops, sugar and cotton, the first being marginal because of exhausted soils and high labour costs, and the second was threatened by disease and falling prices. By the end of 1963 Antigua's climate and magnificent beaches had earned for the island some 40 modern hotels, an enlarged and modernized airport and a number of secondary industries, including factories for making cornmeal, edible oil and cigarettes. By 1962, through the diversification and development of its economy, the gross domestic product increased from $12·1 million (W.I.) to $22·5 (W.I.) and Antigua moved ahead of the other islands in the Leewards and Windwards in terms of per capita income. Bananas made a major contribution to the economy of St Lucia, St Vincent, Grenada and Dominica. These four islands reached a point where their production equalled that of Jamaica, at one time the unrivalled leader in the banana trade.

But the Leeward and Windward Islands faced special difficulties in their efforts at development. These sprang from their smallness, their lack of mineral resources and of sources of hydro-electric power. There was little will towards co-operation in the development or in the exploitation of limited resources. The aeroplane notwithstanding, the sea remains a barrier rather than a road, and the nation is a concrete visible thing whose borders are clearly defined and easily comprehended. The fragmentation of the archipelago hurt the small islands most of all, engendering isolationism and a petty jealousy that reaches absurdity in the resentment that 12,700 people in Nevis, with an area of 36 square miles, feel at the imperialism of St Kitts, 3 miles across the Narrows, 68 square miles in size with 38,300 people; of the 1,200 people of Barbuda over the dominance of nearby Antigua with its 108 square miles and 53,000 people. Eighteenth-century attitudes make it difficult for these small island communities to understand that social groups of less than 100,000 people, isolated from each other by sea, are handicapped in development by a scarcity of trained leaders, the lack of a cultural focus, a conservative outlook, and an extreme sensitivity to criticism.

The economies of the smaller islands, each taken by itself, are small and simple, providing no basis for independence. The choice lies between being colonies or combining to make a larger unit. Quite apart from economic considerations, it is very difficult to secure good government in units of 80,000 or 100,000 persons crowded together in such a way as to reduce non-comformity or political opposition to the level of personal animosity.

Even the two larger islands, Trinidad and Tobago and Jamaica, are comparatively small, and economists are beginning to point out that under-development and sustained growth cannot be considered in isolation from the size of a particular country. Perhaps no other part of the world with the same land area has suffered so much as the Caribbean from fragmentation and attachment to a number of metropolitan powers. It is of interest to contrast the position of Cuba, ten times as large as Jamaica, but deficient in sources of power and with a population of 7 million, which appears to be too small to support a wide range of industrial development.[127] The Castro régime at first attempted industrialization on the Soviet model of import-substitution with emphasis on basic industries as against consumer goods. In 1963 it switched its emphasis to the utilization of domestic raw materials as the basis for exports of manufacture. Jamaica is much smaller than Cuba. Its recently published five-year plan shows realism and courageous effort, but it also illustrates the peculiar disadvantages of smallness. Like the Trinidad plan it provides for a slow-down in the rate of the gross domestic product through a slow-down of the rate of growth of its mineral exports, indicates the limits to import-substitution, puts emphasis on the development of manufacturing exports, and points out the difficulties in expanding export agriculture because of lack of markets rather than because output cannot be increased.

There is mounting urgency about the problem of employment, for migration is no longer possible. In the 1950s it had bought time, allowing local efforts at economic development to get under way. The effect of even limited emigration on Jamaica's population can be seen in the fact that if only 20,000 Jamaicans went to the United Kingdom annually, the island's rate of population growth would fall to one-half the present rate; and the population would reach $3\frac{1}{2}$ million people in 2005 and not in 1985.

Since agriculture is so important in the economy of Jamaica, and since the dualism of estate and peasant holding exists in the island in an extreme form, the Jamaica plan gives considerable importance to land use, and provides for pressure on the estate owner to cultivate his land intensively.

As the plans show, both Jamaica and Trinidad will drive ahead with the promotion of exports of manufacture. This will not provide enough jobs for all the unemployed, however, so it will be necessary for the government to undertake large building and public work programmes. This in turn requires 'soft loans' and close collaboration with local and international investors. It is essential that restraint be exercised in spending by upper- and middle-class West Indians. They are unrealistic in expecting from their society the standards of living that they see in the United States and Canada, and there is need for restraint also by those Trade Unions which seek to carry over into less productive sectors the wage levels that prevail in highly productive industrial sectors.

36 In 1962 both Jamaica and Trinidad and Tobago became independent countries. Each recognizes the British Sovereign as Supreme Head of State. A Trinidadian policeman of the post-independence era.

37 (*left to right*) Sir Alexander Bustamante was the founder of the Jamaican Labour Party. He was the fir[st] chief Minister of Jamaica. Later, in 1962, he became his country's first Prime Minister. 38 Sir Grantley Adam[s] Leader of the Barbados Labour Party and at one time Premier of Barbados. He was Prime Minister of t[he] Federation of the West Indies from 1958 to 1962. 39 Norman Washington Manley founded the Peopl[e's] National Movement in Jamaica, and was the First Leader of Opposition in Parliament after independenc[e.] 40 Dr Eric Williams, after a brilliant academic career, entered politics, founded the People's National Mov[e]ment in Trinidad, and became first Prime Minister of Trinidad and Tobago in 1962.

41 Trinidad, which has an important tourist industry, is one of the largest islands of the West Indies.

(*right*) Jamaica depends heavily
its export trade. This is part of
wn-town Kingston.

Barbados, like the other is-
ds, has an export economy.
is is the picturesque Careenage
Bridgetown. A modern deeper harbour was opened in
3.

44 (*left above*) Dominica, the largest island of the Windward Group exports 80 per cent of its produce to the United Kingdom. Tobacco is one of these.

45 (*left*) Polishing cocoa beans or 'dancing cocoa'.

46 Each island has its special export crop. Nutmegs are grown in Grenada in the Windward Islands.

47 Sugar is the principal crop of the West Indies. This field of sugar cane is at Trinidad.

48 (*left below*) Rum, once called 'Kill devil', is still a principal export of Barbados, Jamaica and Trinidad.

49 Loading bananas at Dominica. In recent years the Windward Islands have developed an important banana industry, equalling Jamaica in production.

50 Since the 1940s the West Indies have developed many new industries. This cement factory is in Jamaica.

51 The discovery of bauxite gave strong support to Jamaica's economy. Mining for bauxite in Jamaica.

52 The refining of asphalt is one of Trinidad's special industries. This liquid pitch is being poured into barrels for export.

53 Fishing is an important industry in many of the islands.

54 (*left*) The people of the West Indies are of mixed racial types. The ancestors of this East Indian girl were probably East Indians taken into Trinidad during the nineteenth century as contract labourers.

55 (*right*) A very large part of the population are of African origin, as a result of the importation of numbers of Africans during the seventeenth and eighteenth centuries.

56 (*left*) This is a student of the University of the West Indies. 57 (*right*) White people form a small minority in the population of the West Indies.

10   Family, Church and School

IN THE ISLANDS there are several forms of family organization,[128] the most important being legal marriage, concubinage or common-law marriage and the single mother with one or more children. Generally legal marriage is according to Christian rites. In Trinidad and Guyana, where there are large East Indian communities, it may be according to Hindu rites. The different forms grew out of the colonial relationship and plantation slavery, and in the case of East Indians, out of the sugar plantation and indentured labour.

In the lands from which the European came monogamous marriage had been traditional for centuries. There were sanctions against adultery. Bastardy carried a stigma. The laws enforced monogamy. The common ethic was Christian. Children were born of a union blessed by the Church. Even the convulsive changes produced by the industrial revolution, the rapid growth of towns, the rise of a proletariat, the dislocation of family life and the rupture of long established social relationships in country and town did not greatly weaken the traditional form of family organization.

The white colonist abandoned this form in the radically altered circumstances of a society based on plantation slavery. In the West Indies of the seventeenth and eighteenth centuries white women were comparatively few and generally faded. The white man was dominant and so had privileges of power which he did not possess in England or in France. He could mate at will with brown and black women. Concubinage and promiscuity became general. Words like adultery, bastard and illegitimate ceased to have any real meaning, save in so far as the inheritance of property was involved.

Descriptions of the West Indies in the eighteenth century show an almost complete abandonment by the white colonists of marriage and of monogamy. Concubinage was 'the custom of the country'. In his *Civil and Natural History of Jamaica*, published in 1789, Patrick Browne referred to the 'great attachments to Negro women; there being but few gentlemen but what have several of those ladies very early in keeping'. Poyer, in his *History of Barbados*, tells how, while Ricketts was Governor of Barbados, a Negro woman resided in Government House, enjoying all the privileges of a wife apart from presiding publicly at meals. Lady Nugent, whose *Journal* describes life in Jamaica during her husband's governorship, between 1801 and 1805, says that many in her service claimed to be daughters of members of the House of Assembly or of officers, and that they took pride in their parentage. When she visited Hope Estate, near Kingston, she talked with

'the overseer's chère amie, and no man here is without one, a tall black woman, well made, with a very flat nose, thick lips and a skin of ebony, highly polished and shining. She showed me her three yellow children, and said with some ostentation that she would soon have another. The marked attention of the other women plainly proved her to be the favourite Sultana of this vulgar, ugly Scotch Sultan, who is about fifty, clumsy, ill-made and dirty. . . .'

Edward Waller, a naval officer, in his *Voyage to the West Indies*, tells of a respectable lady, 'a virgin, between fifty and sixty', who had let out a young female slave to an officer for 12 dollars a month. The officer was leaving the island, if Waller would have her, she would abate her price somewhat. Waller was 'extremely shocked at the idea of so strange a traffic', possibly because he was a newcomer. A few days later he saw the girl advertised in the following curious terms:

'To let: a seamstress, a well-looking mulatto girl, seventeen years of age, an excellent hand at her needle, etc. To prevent needless application, terms, twelve dollars a month.'

The married white man usually kept one or two mistresses, and raised families 'on the side'. In some instances legitimate and illegitimate children, 'house children' and 'yard children', lived together in the same household. In his diary the Revd. William Jones, writing at the end of the eighteenth century, records that Mr H. told him with an oath that he was amazed that men formed any other than black and brown connections in Jamaica; that few marriages lasted and that the husband often returned 'to his former acquaintance, to wallow in the mire of sensuality which old and young, married and single in this accursed country would fain believe always allowable'.

What mattered in these unions was not morality but colour. Bryan Edwards says that mulatto girls were kept as mistresses by white men of all ranks, but that 'no White Man of decent appearance, unless urged by the temptation of a considerable fortune, will condescend to give his hand in marriage to a mulatto. The very idea is shocking'. Pigmentation determined prestige and power, so, from the woman's point of view, mating with a white man held the promise of greater benefit for her children. It was possible to 'raise one's colour' by careful mating, but the road to whitedom, and therefore to acceptance, was a long one, demanding a selectivity beyond the reach of passion. Monk Lewis, in his *Journal*, noted the gradations: the offspring of a white man and a black woman is a mulatto; the mulatto and black produce a sambo; from a mulatto and white comes the quadroon; from the quadroon and white comes the mustee; the child of a mustee by a white man is called a musteefino, while the children of a musteefino are free by law and rank as white persons to all intents and purposes.

On the slave plantation concubinage became traditional for black as well as white.[129] In his own country, and amongst his own tribal communities, the African had been subject to elaborate procedures governing mating relationships through kinship or lineage groups, with the ceremonial exchange of property, and the incorporation of children into a fixed line of descent. But in the Caribbean these long-established procedures could not be established. Each slave was a single piece of property, and being property he was forbidden to marry. A man and woman belonging to the same estate were free to mate, but mating relationships were unstable and the offspring were neither legitimate nor illegitimate. In the context of slavery these words had no meaning. Children were the lawful property of the owner of the slave mother, and the master was free to dispose of them at will.

'Under these conditions the woman normally acted as the sole permanent element in the slave family. . . . Normally the children resided with their mother, and the parents lived apart, singly or with different mates, but instances of slave parents living with their children are also reported.'[130]

The census figures throw light on the present position. The marital status of women is shown under four headings: single mothers, that is, women who have borne a child but who were single at the time of the census; common-law marriage, the term covering a man and woman who lived together without having been legally married; the married and the widowed. The figures reveal a remarkable likeness between all the English-speaking islands except for Trinidad, in spite of the many cultural and economic differences between them.

Only about one-third of the women with marital status were married. About one-third were single mothers. The number of illegitimate births ranged from almost 60 per cent in Barbados to 70 per cent in St Vincent. This is a legal classification, which does not take into account the stability of many common-law marriages; but the figures show that instability of mating patterns and of family organization is among the most urgent social problems of the West Indies.

Sociologists are generally agreed that the main functioning family unit in the Caribbean is the household group. The household is larger than the immediate family, including one or more grandparents, relatives on both sides, cousins and even more distant kin. In his study, *The Negro Family in British Guiana*, Smith describes the household as coming into being when a man and woman set up house together as man and wife. They may already have been 'friends' or lovers, and indeed may have children, the woman providing the man with sexual services in return for economic support, 'but until they live together there is no explicit recognition of the man's exclusive right to her sexual services'.

This extension or widening of the family is reflected in the speech of the lower classes. In Jamaica 'talk', the word 'family' is used not only as a noun but also almost in the sense of an adjective meaning 'related to'. 'Me and him is family', means simply that we are rela/ tives. In order to show that bananas and plantains belong to the same species, a farmer may say, 'banana is family to plantain'. Another phrase often used to describe relationship is 'fe we', that is, 'for we, for us, of our family or kin'. 'Anybody fe we' means 'anyone who is of our family'. The relationship extends into the spirit world: 'Care must be taken in throwing out water at night to warn the family spirits who may be near. "Mind yourselves, me family", or "good people", they cry, or "Anybody fe we, move".'

The household based on common/law marriage is strongly mother/centred, with a close relationship between mother, daughter and grand/daughter. The man's status and authority largely depend on his power to support the household. Dr Raymond Smith has emphasized that this type of family system, with its three generation matriline and with women in a central position of authority is closely related to low status and seasonal or casual employment.[131]

Trinidad presents a special case because of its large East Indian community. The East Indians who were brought to the Guianas and to Trinidad between 1850 and 1920 came from a society in which marriage was permanent with neither divorce nor the re/marriage of widows allowed by Hinduism. Brides were selected by the parents, child marriage was the rule, the woman was subordinate in the household, the father as head of the family made the decisions, and families were expected to stay together indefinitely. The immigrants went from this kind of society in their own country on to West Indian plantations whose owners or managers were concerned only with getting the maximum amount of work out of them. The plantation system paid no regard to the home life of its workers. On the cane fields distinctions of caste were of no account. Women and men worked together in a system that produced overwork and immorality. Nevertheless the East Indians, through their common language, their religion and the service of their own priests, rebuilt in Trinidad and Guyana a way of life based on the forms and values of India. For all East Indians, whether first or third generation, India is the mother country, not in the sense in which the educated West Indian spoke of Britain, but because it is the ancestral home, the society to which they belong naturally through birth, religion, language, history. Trinidad therefore, is culturally more complex and racially more divided than any other West Indian country. The national motto 'Together we aspire', describes with great accuracy the central task that confronts East and West Indian Trinidadians of finding a national unity despite basic differences of race and culture. East Indians and West Indian creoles live together side by side, within one political unit in a plural society such as that of Burma or Malaya. In those lands the culturally distinct groups are aware of, and appear to accept, the pluralistic nature of their societies. In Trinidad this would be true of the East Indian, but from the Trinidad West Indian point of view the island contains an essentially homogeneous society; if it did not it should and soon would. The creole accepts integration and assimilation as a national goal. His social values are largely based on colour and race, pointing with pride to the fact that he has 'English', 'Spanish', 'French' blood in his veins. This is not the case with the East Indian. Though he looks on Trinidad as his home, he is also an Indian. The East Indian working man who has saved up for a holiday in Barbados or a race meeting in Tobago returns with pleasure to his island, saying to the friends who meet him, 'Boy, it's a beauty to be in Trinidad again'. But he sees himself also as an East Indian. Racially and culturally he identifies himself with India. In his Trinidad village or township his values are determined by caste and religion rather than by the traditional West Indian colour scale.

'The West Indian may be said to be striving to become more European, or at least more creole, and less African. The East Indian may like his circumstances to be bettered, but he has no desire to be anything else, and least of all a West Indian.'[132]

The pattern of family organization and the social values inculcated through child training in the family differentiate the two groups.[133]

122

As in India, East Indian women marry young. Many of the marriages are arranged by the parents. Marriages are carried through with the customary religious rites, sometimes by a priest who is an accredited marriage officer, sometimes by one who is not; and on occasion even the marriage officer may have neglected to fulfil the legal require, ments. These marriages therefore are more easily dissolved than Christian marriages, and investigation indicates that the East Indian marriages contracted between the ages of 15 and 20 are less stable than those contracted between 20 and 25 or than the Christian mar, riages among non-Indians. Braithwaite and Roberts, in a study of mating among East Indian and non-East Indian women, found that 90 per cent of East Indian women were married by the age of 25 whereas the proportion at the same age among non-Indian women was 31 per cent. By the age of 45 only three out of 100 East Indian women were unmarried, as against approximately 33 per cent non-Indian women. Among non-Indian women 'visiting', that is, regular sexual intercourse between a man and woman who do not live together, and unions in which a man and woman live together without marriage are much more common than among Indian women. For East Indian women marriage dominates the initial stage; the other two union types are in general of only marginal significance.

> 'The importance of marriage in the mating experience of East Indians emerges from the fact that they pass on the average 20·4 years, or about 66 per cent of the child-bearing span, in such unions. By contrast marriage accounts for less than one-third of the child-bearing span, or about 9·6 years, in the case of women of other races.'[134]

Among non-Indian women marriage is less frequent, 'visiting' and common-law marriage more frequent; and marriage in any case is, on the average, seven or eight years later. It follows that the East Indian child is more likely to grow up in a family in which the father is present than the non-Indian child.

The strength of East Indian family life can be judged from the census figures; but it appears in the shape of flesh and blood in every village and town in the Trinidad sugar belt. Along the flatland east of Port-of-Spain, at Aranjuez, East Indian market-gardeners grow vegetables for sale, tomatoes, aubergines, cucumbers, pumpkins, leeks, escallion, squash, sweet peppers, cabbages. At planting time, father, mother, grandmother and eight or ten children work together, bent over the land, moulding it with their hands and their hoes, shaping, planting, weeding with delicate care, pre-occupied, intent on earning money to buy bread and pay the rent. While the plants grow the family fights off insects, and father and son live in a shack in the field at harvest-time to protect their labour against thieves. The curse of the father may not carry the dread weight that it does in India but few in an East Indian family question the authority of the father or the bidding of the mother. Those who disobey 'get licks'. Smiles come quickly to the soft-voiced children with flashing black eyes, the girls with pigtails of long black hair carefully combed and plaited, and glossy with coconut oil; but there is an almost frightening intensity in the combination of back-breaking labour and singleness of purpose. The weight of tradition is written on the young brown body of a small girl carrying a pail of water, and in the posture of a boy of six weeding a patch of cabbages, each carrying out its task, accomplishing its work, making the family secure.

'East Indians are orientated to the past by their religious and caste heritage, and toward the future by their interest in material security and accumulation. Negroes are used to a wide range of social interaction and are sensitive to public opinion whereas East Indians are concerned with the family and restricted social relationships.'[135]

Religion played a powerful part in helping the East Indian indentured labourer to rebuild his way of life and to retain his respect for the Brahmin and Kshattriya castes in a foreign land with other values. But the slave plantation destroyed the religious system of the African, and it refused him any share in Christianity before the rise of the evangelical movement and the founding of missionary societies.

Up to the beginning of the nineteenth century the established Anglican Church ministered to established authority and wealth.

Its clergy were appointed by the Governor. Some of them were pious men at a disadvantage in a grossly materialistic society where the churches were filled only for funerals; others, wrote the historian Edward Long, were better qualified to be retailers of codfish, boat-swains, or privateers. Among these was the Revd. William Davis of St Kitts, parson and estate-property manager, who was indicted for the murder of Eliza, a slave woman.

The parish churches were the symbols of planter power and of the established order, rather than centres of religious enthusiasm. The description left by Lady Nugent of a visit to a church service in Black River, capital of one of the parishes of Jamaica, is in line with accounts by other visitors. The clergyman's wife excused herself from attending on account of the service being so long, and her daughter, the widow of the late Chief Justice did the same; at the communion there were only 'one old white man and woman and one brown lady beside ourselves'.[136]

The preaching of Wesley and Whitfield and the rise of missionary societies took Christianity to the slave. In 1794 Bishop Porteus founded a society in London for the conversion and education of the slaves, and the first half of the nineteenth century presents remarkable progress by Baptist and Methodist missionaries who worked on the plantations in the islands, teaching and educating the slaves, founding schools and later establishing free villages. Through these missionaries the Bible became the book of the West Indian peasant, influencing his phraseology and vocabulary. The older people still use words like 'peradventure' and 'hand-maiden', and quote Old Testament verses to justify belief in visions and spirits, the keeping of concubines, and in justification of large families repeat the injunction to go forth and multiply.

In the West Indies of today the influence of the Christian religion is strong. In Trinidad, Grenada, St Lucia and Dominica, which were Spanish or French for a time, the Roman Catholic Church is very powerful. In Trinidad also many East Indians remain faithful to Hinduism or to Islam, and there are a number of Hindu primary schools. The older sugar islands, Barbados, Jamaica and the Lee-ward Islands are predominantly Protestant. In these the Anglican

Church claims the largest membership, with the Baptist and Methodist Churches close behind; and there are in addition Moravians, Presbyterians, Congregationalists, Churches of Christ, Seventh Day Adventists, Jehovah Witnesses and a number of other sects.

On the slave estates there was another presence, known sometimes through drummings and midnight meetings, and the use of magic to bring about spirit possession, divination, healing and death. The Vodun of Haiti, the remnants of Obi in Jamaica and of Shango in Trinidad point to the transfer of elements of African religion to the islands, and many of the religious cults and revivalist movements of the West Indies show a mingling of both the African and Christian religions. A recent study of Shango in Trinidad[137] shows that the cult is confined to a relatively small number of uneducated lowerclass people, mainly of darkskin colour. They worship and invoke powers that have African and Catholic names, like Abatal or St Benedict, and Ogun or St Michael. Each 'power', has his own special characteristic. Shango is the God of thunder and lightning, and the sacrifice due to him is a red or a white cock, or pigeons; Oshun is Mistress of the Ocean and rates a female goat or hen; Oya, the mistress of the wind and rain is hottempered, 'like a hurricane'. Dreams, visions and possession by the spirits have an important part in this cult, as in Obi and Vodun. Drumming and singing for a power are the most important immediate stimuli which precipitate possession. As with Obi, the multiple soulconcept of West Africa has been retained, with the belief that in addition to a soul a dead person has a shadow that remains behind after death, and if it is not properly dismissed, 'disturbs people'. The wakes that are often held in the islands nine nights after death are the occasions for dismissing the shadow or spirit and putting it to rest.[138]

Religion is an essential part of everyday life in the West Indies. Among many uneducated people the spirit world is real and spirits intervene in human affairs through visions, dreams and other forms of guidance. One result of this is an acceptance of things as they are. A man fails in business not because he is incompetent but through the trickery of a neighbour or for some reason outside of himself. But the deep sense of supernatural powers may also produce protest and there were often close links between slave rituals and slave risings. In the nineteenth century the leader of the 1865 protest against injustice, often mistakenly termed the Jamaica rebellion, was a Baptist deacon. In the 1831 rising of slaves in Jamaica the central figure was a Baptist deacon called Daddy Sharp.

From time to time messianic cults arose around some leader of strong personality, such as the prophet Bedward in Jamaica in the 1920s. These cults tend rapidly to become movements.

The most remarkable of these cults is the Ras Tafari movement in Jamaica.[139] It seems to have been inspired by Garvey's 'Back to Africa' Campaign. Reports say that he told his people: 'Look to Africa, when a black king shall be crowned, for the day of deliverance is near'. In November 1930, Ras Tafari was crowned as the Emperor Haile Selassie. Jamaicans who believed in Garvey searched their Bibles, and found confirmation of his message in the Book of Revelation: 'Weep not, behold the Lion of Judah, the Root of David hath prevailed to open the Book'. Ras Tafari was the Lion of Judah. In the Bible they found also that Mussolini's attack on Ethiopia was foretold: 'I saw the Beast, and the Kings of the Earth gathered together and their armies gathered together to make war against him that sat on the horse'. The defeat of the Italians and the return of the Emperor were also foretold: 'And the Beast was taken, and with him the false prophet. . . . These both were cast alive into a lake of fire burning with brimstone.'

In 1934 a small group of men and women, recalling Garvey's prophecy about a king crowned in Africa, recognized Haile Selassie as the Living God and became his followers, the Ras Tafari. This cult holds two basic doctrines; that Haile Selassie is divine, and that salvation comes only to those black men who are repatriated to Africa and live under black government. The way of the white man is rejected as evil. The language of the movement is often violent for it is the language of the Old Testament. From time to time criminal elements have joined the Ras Tafari, inciting them to wrongdoing. Some of 'the brethren' grow and take the 'weed', marijuana, or Indian hemp. But the great majority are peaceful people who join the movement to escape from the shiftless despair of unemployment.

'The movement is rooted in unemployment. . . . If the supply of jobs in Kingston were to catch up with the demand for jobs, a hard core of religious belief would remain but the movement would cease to have mass significance.'[140]

Cults like Shango and the Ras Tafari movement result from the intermingling of two worlds that met in the Caribbean four and a half centuries ago but which have not yet merged together. They reveal some of the tensions in West Indian society; the search for self-expression through religion and the creation of a mythology; a passionate striving for a world in which blackness is linked with achievement and position; and the rejection of a society in which men find only the frustrations of poverty and unemployment.

The various forms of family organization and of religion differentiate the two chief sections in West Indian society: an upper and middle class with a family structure based on formal marriage, and with attachments to orthodox Christianity; and the mass of the population, in some islands comprising four out of every five persons, among whom the matrifocal household described earlier in this chapter is the rule, with attachments to those Christian Churches that are revivalist in character, and to a number of religious cults.

In these circumstances, West Indian nationalism became a search for unity as well as for economic security, and this search led to education. The West Indian governments have had to undertake this search against a deadline, for the existence of political democracy and party government has produced demands for immediate action in a score of directions, and electorates newly enfranchised, actively reaching out for a better way of life after a century of apathy, want everything and want it now.

Priority has been given to education. Trinidad has oil and people, Jamaica bauxite and people, Barbados and the other islands, people. Since people constitute the chief, and in many instances the only, resource, they have to be educated as rapidly as possible.

Three objectives govern the expansion and development of education: the rejection of the colonial policy of providing elementary education for the masses and secondary education for a small *élite*;

128

changes in the content of education so as to make it relevant; and the provision of university training within the region.

Through a long association with Britain, the West Indian system of education follows the English pattern. Elementary schools take children from seven to 14 years old, secondary schools from 12 to 18. Up to 1947 those who wished to attend university had to go overseas.

The level of attainment varies from island to island. It is remarkably high in Barbados where 98 per cent of the population has had some schooling, and 58 per cent have completed the elementary school course. In Trinidad and Tobago the corresponding proportions are 87 per cent and 51 per cent; in Jamaica 16 per cent and 53 per cent. These figures indicate that the English-speaking islands are in a much better position than many of the neighbouring countries, such as the Dominican Republic where only 30 per cent of the population has had formal schooling. Haiti is badly placed, for 90 per cent of its people have had no schooling.

Up to 1940 a very small number of children of school age attended secondary school. This was traditional, for the state school system of the islands reinforced the class structure by keeping rigid barriers between primary and secondary levels and by maintaining the orientation of the English public school. In 1869 a searching assessment of education in Trinidad led to a proposal that sets of Irish Readers then commonly in use should be replaced by readers containing lessons 'racy of the colony'. The Report expressed surprise at the fact that while the white population of the island, between 5,000 and 6,000 in number, furnished 142 pupils to the secondary schools, the coloured population of 60,000 (excluding East Indians) furnished only 24 pupils. Evidence given before a Select Committee of the Legislative Council of Trinidad included the statement by a planter that 'This is an agricultural country; unless you put the children on to working in the fields when they are young you will never get them to do so later'. In Jamaica, at an earlier date, Olivier noted that there had always prevailed among the upper classes the view that 'book learning' was useless and deleterious to a black population.[141] In Jamaica as late as the 1930s only one out of every 80 children of school age received secondary schooling.

The quantity of secondary education was too small for a develop-ing country. But, what was far more serious, the little was distributed unequally. It was shared out according to the ability to pay. This had the effect of deepening the cleavages in West Indian society, for the majority, the black people, were in occupations that had the lowest status and were most poorly paid, whereas the comparatively small white group were in better paid occupations. The sickness of West Indian society can be measured by the census figures of 1943 and 1948, the period in which the first constitutional reforms were introduced. The three groups in the West Indian population, black, brown and white were differentiated by education, conjugal con-dition, family organization, religious institutions and economic institutions. In 1943 in Jamaica 98 per cent of the black population had only elementary education, 0·9 per cent secondary, and 0·1 per cent professional training. Just over 87 per cent of the coloured group had only elementary schooling, 8·7 per cent secondary, and 0·8 per cent professional training. Of the white group 37·9 per cent had elementary education, 47 per cent secondary and 5·6 professional training. In the Eastern Caribbean at the same period the percentage of illiteracy in the racial groups in the Leeward Islands was 6 per cent among the whites, 9 per cent among the coloured and 16 per cent among the blacks. In all the islands, the literacy rate was highest among the whites, lower among the coloured, lowest among the blacks. The same gradations were found in the occupations; a large concentration of black people at the lower end of the scale in occupa-tions such as agricultural and general labour and domestic service, and a large concentration of whites at the upper end, where the occupations required skilled people. The educational system and the distribution of educational opportunity perpetuated these inequalities.

Besides, there was a marked difference in the quality of education received. The secondary schools reached a high level. Dr Eric Williams, writing of the secondary school to which he won a government scholarship in Port-of-Spain, said that one of the island scholars of 1911 was placed first among 57 candidates in the British Empire in agricultural science; of 83 students who gained distinc-tions in history four were from Trinidad. At the 1910 examinations

one island scholar was placed first in the Senior Cambridge Exam,
inations throughout the Empire. W. J. Locke, island scholar for
1879, became a successful novelist. Another scholar for 1884 became
Sir Robert Falconer, President of the University of Toronto. The
record of this school was not far different from that of the leading
secondary schools in Barbados, Guyana and Jamaica. But in general,
conditions in the elementary schools were unsatisfactory with
inadequate buildings, few books, crowded classes of from 50 to 100
children, a large number of untrained teachers and pupil teachers. As
late as 1950 a visitor found that:

> 'at worst the schools are places where the children learn everything
> parrot fashion with frequent beatings when they make mistakes, at
> the best they are places where teachers with genuine enthusiasm for
> education struggle against the most appalling odds to get their
> ideals across.'[142]

In both secondary and elementary schools the content of education
was unsuited to West Indian conditions. One result was that many
children never learned to begin to sort out the world of reality for
themselves since the world of the book was so different from their
own world. At the secondary school level students turned their faces
away from their own way of life to that of a distant country, con,
cerning whose Plantagenet and Tudor Kings they learned a number
of unpleasant facts. It was assumed that the West Indies had no
history, and that the inhabitants of Cuba, Puerto Rico and the other
Caribbean islands were at a lower level of civilization. Toussaint
was a rebel who deserved his fate, the name of Marti was unknown,
and Bolivar was a man of no standing whose head deluded Latin
Americans occasionally put on postage stamps. The more intelligent
the student the more natural it was that he should be fired by the
struggles and victories of England, by the exploits of Drake and
Nelson, the establishment of liberty and parliamentary government
in the face of the opposition of kings, the fierce passion for freedom
that in the end swept Napoleon to defeat at Waterloo. Noble pas,
sages of literature were learned by heart and treasured. But what did
the West Indies have to offer apart from the shames and agonies of

131

slavery? The Ghanaian knew that he belonged to people with their own history; the educated West Indian adopted the history and the heroes of another land.

As soon as the West Indian governments began to assume greater political responsibility they began to change the educational struc‑ ture, opening the secondary schools to those with ability rather than to those with means. The policy of Trinidad and Tobago is free secondary education for every child. Jamaica is seeking to provide 80 per cent of its child population with secondary education. The story is the same throughout the West Indies. Generous action by the British Parliament in establishing a Development and Welfare Fund made possible the erection of new schools and technical colleges and provided large capital funds for the establishment of a university, for by the 1940s the old colonial concept and the will to empire had reached the death‑bed stage.

The secondary school population is increasing rapidly. In Jamaica it jumped from 7,000 in 1951 to 19,000 in 1960. Barbados has the highest proportion of those who have had secondary schooling, 16 per cent; Trinidad and Tobago have 14 per cent. For the other islands the figures are lower; 7 per cent for Jamaica, 8 per cent for Grenada and only 2 per cent in St Lucia. Only a comparatively small proportion of the population has had secondary school training at the upper level and taken the School Certificate or Higher School Certificate examinations: 5 per cent in Barbados and Jamaica, 4 per cent in Trinidad and Tobago and 2 per cent to 3 per cent in the other islands. As far as higher education is concerned, in 1960 only 0·7 per cent of the population of Trinidad and Tobago had received university education.[143] Barbados was next with 0·6 per cent. In most of the other islands, including Jamaica, the percentage was 0·3 per cent, whereas it is 3 per cent in the neighbouring island of Puerto Rico which is more highly industrialized.

'The extent to which the Caribbean as a whole falls short of the standards of the industrial countries is revealed by the fact that in Canada 8 per cent of its population has had university training and in the United States 13 per cent are so qualified.'[144]

The cost is heavy, the time is short, for the governments are all work-ing against a deadline. A 'birth line' would be more accurate. It has been estimated that between 1960 and 1975 the population of all the West Indian islands and of Guyana will have increased by nearly 2 million; the population of overcrowded Barbados by a third, rising to 312,000: Jamaica by three-quarters of a million to 2·3 million; Trinidad and Tobago by a half, to 1·2 million. The birth-rates for Jamaica and Barbados appear to have stabilized themselves, standing now at 31·9 and 32·1 per thousand respectively, but the fertility rate in Trinidad and Guyana with their large East Indian communities is high and shows no sign of decline. Though there has been much heavier government spending on education, with the erection of more primary and secondary schools and provision for technical and university education, there are large numbers of children for whom there is no adequate provision.

There have been important advances in technical education. Tech-nical high schools and Colleges of Arts, Science and Technology have been established. In Jamaica agricultural and vocational education has been increased through the establishment of practical training centres located in rural areas. The best West Indian school of agriculture at the pre-university level is in Jamaica at Twickenham Park, about 8 miles west of Kingston. It trains pupils for work on properties as overseers or technical officers. The course of study extends over three years, and combines theoretical work with a good deal of practical work on a large modern farm.

The establishment of a university in the West Indies would have been delayed if there had not been strong urging and support from the United Kingdom. There was in Jamaica, in 1942, a small com-mittee of citizens working for the founding of a university, but they had no financial backing and met local opposition. It was a symp-tom of the dissociation of West Indian intellectuals from the society that many of the *élite* who had been educated abroad questioned the advisability of establishing a local university. The plans for the University College of the West Indies were prepared on the initia-tive of the British government, which provided the capital money for buildings and equipment. Over the years, taking into account

133

expansion in Trinidad and Barbados, this has reached the sum of £10 million. The West Indian governments meet the recurrent cost through a University Grants Committee as in Britain but with this difference, that in Britain one Committee deals with a large number of universities whereas in the West Indies many govern, ments deal with one university.

The University was planned as a residential university aiming at an enrolment of 500 students and insisting from the start on high academic standards, and it sought to secure this objective through a special relationship with the University of London. In 1960 radical changes were made in the policy of the University. A campus was started in Trinidad, and in 1962 another was started in Barbados. The residential requirement was thrown overboard. Governments provided more scholarships. Evening programmes of study were begun. Graduate work was encouraged. As a result, student num, bers rose from 1,000 in 1960 to 3,100 in 1965. The University is fully autonomous, giving its own diplomas, certificates and advanced degrees.

But how does the 'borrowed instrument' become a West Indian one? In what ways can a university, which is faced with the urgent task of establishing itself as a worthy centre of research and teaching, remain sensitive to the many needs of the people it serves and the governments that support it? In a society in which secondary and university education have been divisive how does it secure identifi, cation and devotion?[144] How does it institutionalize science and scholarship in a region where there is no great tradition, where the dominant motives were commercial, and the chief method was the en, slavement of human beings? By what means does it build excellence and a respect for human personality in a society more deeply seamed by colour differences than a steel drum is by the lines that give tone? How does it bring down the cost of education in a society where glaring inequalities of income have marked the difference between educated and uneducated? How are West Indian teachers and research workers, trained in the philosophy of the *élite* and accus, tomed to United Kingdom salary scales, to understand that small developing countries have to get from their educated people more scholarship and productive effort, more yield per brain at lower cash cost?

Slowly and with effort the answers are being found. The role of the social and natural sciences is being emphasized, numbers have been increased, required courses have been added to the curriculum, and there is conscious concern about the West Indian university student as a social product, one who has some idea of and commitment to his country, and who can place his country in some historical perspective.

11 Folklore and Custom

IN ADDITION TO standard English, each of the islands has its own creole language, the word 'creole' being used to mean 'island born'. In Grenada, St Lucia, Dominica and parts of St Vincent the creole language is French patois, similar to that of Martinique and Haiti. The Trinidad creole language is strongly influenced by Spanish and French, with a number of constructions based on French. A Trinidadian who feels unwell may say, 'I have bad feelings', and if there is water in the jug, he may say, 'They have in the jug'.

The creole language[145] owes little to the indigenous people of the islands. Since they survived longer in Trinidad than in many of the other West Indian islands, more Amerindian placenames remain in use, like Piarco, the island's international airport, and Arima, Curepe, Tunapuna; but the influence of the Amerindian on West Indian folk talk is negligible. The two chief components are English of different kinds and African of different kinds.

Many of the first white settlers were people of little education, artisans, impoverished tenants, servants. Some of the latter were Scots taken in the wars against Cromwell and transported, or men convicted of vagrancy and other offences; Irish captured in Cromwell's merciless harrying of their country; Welshmen and West Country men. These carried into the islands old English words and usages that survive in the creole, words like 'gawky', 'mickle/muckle', 'dandy/shandy'; the use of the word 'evening' for anytime after three o'clock in the day, 'beast' for a mule or horse, 'fowl' in preference to chicken; island people still speak of 'stone fence', and use words like 'gat' and 'gut' to denote an opening and a gulley: Flowers do not 'bloom' but 'blow' as they did once in England; 'Breadkind' is food.

136

To accompany one along the road is 'to carry him a part of the way'; to arrive at a place is 'to catch at' it.

Since the sea is the chief character in Caribbean history, and the arrival of ships was a matter of great importance, nautical words became a part of island speech; and the steadiness with which the trade winds blow from the northeast throughout the year led to the use of 'windward and leeward'. Seafaring people, like the Caymanians, use the cardinal points of the compass in giving directions, going into the northeast room of a house or fetching a book from the shelf at the southeast corner. It is reported that in the early days of sugarmaking in Jamaica a slave-driver at the sugar mill was called the 'Boatswain of the mill'; starting the mill was 'to rig' it or to 'put it about'. Cassidy, in *Jamaica Talk*, goes on to say that an estate with an ample supply of labour was 'well handed' and one with few workers 'bad handed'; and he noted that sometimes the sea word 'cookhouse' was preferred to 'kitchen'.

The other main stream of influence was African. At first sight it seems strange that the African element in the folk speech is not stronger than it is, since Africans were brought to the West Indies by the thousand, year after year, for a century and a half. Unlike the East Indians, they had many languages, came from many different nations and tribes, and were transported and sold as individuals and not by the family or tribal group. It was the policy to separate them as much as possible so as to make slave risings more difficult. The slaves had to find a common language in order to communicate with each other and with the European. In a compact island like Barbados, which had a relatively large white group, many of the newly imported slaves soon learned English. A report on conditions in the island in the 1660s said that there were so many white servants in the island and so many poor whites who worked in the fields, and so many Negroes who had become tradesmen, that there were thousands of slaves who spoke English.

Because Jamaica is a much larger island, and had a smaller proportion of white persons, the African influence on the language is stronger than in the creole English of Barbados. The Maroons, many of whom were Coromanti people, retained elements of their

137

Twi-language for a longer period than did the slaves on the estates. Cassidy, in *Jamaica Talk*, points out that African influence affected pronunciation and grammar, as well as vocabulary. He claims that about 230 words from various African languages survive. This number is small in proportion to the English words, yet it appears that the African element is larger than all the other non-English ones put together. Most of the African loan words are the names of plants and foods, of customs and beliefs that belonged to the everyday life of the slave on the plantation; plants like ackee and a kind of yam called 'afu', 'fufu' for crushed yam and 'gungu' for a variety of pea; 'akra' for cakes or fritters made from codfish; 'duckoonoo', a heavy sort of pone; 'bankra' for basket, 'duppy' or 'jumby' for spirit.

There is in the character and mood of the creole language much that is African rather than European, for it was spoken and fashioned by generations of Africans who worked on the plantations or in the towns, did all the manual labour, produced sugar, fetched and carried and slowly rooted themselves in lands once alien. The physical setting shaped the way of life. In cold countries life is driven indoors and statements are muted. But in warm countries the sun draws life out, bringing cuttings of bougainvillaea and oleander to flower within a year, banana suckers and joints of sugar-cane to bursting maturity within nine or ten months of planting. There is no declension of the sun. Flowers and fruit, crop time and planting time, rain and drought mark the seasons; for winter, scarlet poinsettia and steel-grey plumes of sugar-cane; for spring, the tender purples and greens of young mango leaves and the smell of fermenting fields brown from reaping; cascades of yellow cassia and golden logwood blossoms for summer; and for autumn the smell of the first showers on parched fields and the intense green of plants and shrubs exploding into leaf.

The sun draws life into the open, from inner rooms to the shade of a breadfruit tree in the yard, from the yard on to the side roads where, in the morning in Trinidad, East Indian women spread husked rice to dry and in the afternoon boys play cricket, their brown and black bodies gleaming in the sunshine; where at dusk in a Jamaican village a band of white-robed revivalists gather for a preaching; and at high noon in Grenada an old woman breaks stones and a man shouts a greeting to his neighbour while yet almost out of sight. In cold countries a road is used for travel but in warm countries for living. Life is lived out of doors, catching colour from the sun. Against the background of valleys and mountains, as in a theatre without walls, gesture becomes a part of language, amplifying, intensifying, vivifying. Abstractions take on bodies. The world has no half-tones, no twilight, but darkness or light.

In this setting language comes alive with gentle whimsy, a shaft of ridicule, flashing scorn, full-bellied laughter. The quality is not simply that of imagery but a way of concretizing thought, personify-ing it in the way that Africa does, through the visual and through the symbolism of sound. Many of the names given to places and to things have this pictorial quality. Some names are descriptive of the nature of the country, like the Land of Look Behind, an almost impen-etrable region of razor-sharp limestone pinnacles, hidden caves and tangled bush in which the Maroons took refuge; Wait-a-Bit, Come-See, Time-and-Patience, Fruitful Vale, Starve Gut Bay and Pin-nacle. The country bus that passes through on its way to market, laden with baskets, sacks and men and women is Gaiety, Western Pride, Star of the East, Princess Royal. Names enter the realm of fantasy in Trinidad where a Calypsonian becomes Lord High-Executioner, Mighty Sparrow, Mighty Dictator, Mighty Panther, Lord Superior.

Other names and epithets gain their effect from the sound.[146] The word for a man who is utterly worthless and incapable is 'nyamps' the 'ny' sound reflecting a lip curved upwards in contempt. A clumsy fellow is a 'bufu-bufu'. 'Mumu' describes a stupid man, 'fenky-fenky' a fuss-box, 'picky-picky' someone finicking, 'sweet mout' a flatterer; 'big-eye' people are covetous; a 'hard-ears' man is stubborn, 'trickify' is for cunning, 'pyaw-pyaw' for feeble. The name for a bug that attacks the sweet potato before it matures is Mary Grudgeful. The colouring of the ladybird or 'lady bug' wins for it the name 'policeman' because it is blue and red like a policeman's uniform. A variety of wild fig that grows over another tree until at last it swallows it is 'Scotchman' or 'Scotch attorney'; the sensitive plant that folds up its leaves at the lightest touch is 'shame lady', or 'dead-and-wake'; the periwinkle with its strong smell is 'ram-goat dashalong'; the St Vincent yam which gives an early crop and is especially valuable because it propagates itself by seed and does not need to be replanted is 'come-here-fe-help-we yam'; the long smooth okra is 'lady finger'; a tree whose thin flat pods rattle continually in the wind is 'woman's tongue'; the spathodia whose flowers contain a few drops of water is 'water-man'; and the long-tailed humming bird is a 'doctor bird'. Many verbs conjure up images like 'sweet up' meaning to play up to someone; to 'wrap up with', is to be familiar with; to 'work him head', to think out a plan. 'To carry-go-bring-come' means tell-tale, and 'su-su', whispering.

The folk sayings and proverbs glitter with light, like the proverbs of the Akan-Ashanti people, or like the Yoruba riddles, such as that of the cooking pot and the fire:[147]

> *The black one is squatting*
> *The red one is licking his bottom,*

or of dry leaves on the earth, that make a sound when trodden on, whereas the green ones do not:

> *We call the dead, they answer*
> *We call the living, they do not answer.*

The West Indian, like the West African, delights in riddles. Often these begin with a formula: 'Riddle me riddle, riddle me ree, Guess me this riddle and perhaps not, Rope run, horse stand up.' This is a pumpkin on its vine. My father has a house that stands on one post, is an umbrella. My father has a flock of sheep, touch one and the rest die, is the sensitive plant. The parallel to the Yoruba cooking pot and the fire is John Redman tickle John Blackman till he laugh 'pooka pooka'.

The characters in the West Indian proverbs[148] are plants and animals; insects such as the flea, louse, wasp and spider; fish; reptiles like the lizard, snake, alligator, and toad; fowl; birds of many kinds; the dog, cat, mongoose, monkey, puppy, pig and other animals; fruit, vegetables, trees and shrubs. These are the messengers of wis-

dom, reminding us that 'Not because John Crow don't have teeth
you mus' think him can't tear meat'. It is best not to judge by
appearances for 'Alligator lay egg but him no fowl'. Many birds eat
the banana but it is the talkative one that gets blamed: 'Because parrot mek noise dey say is him nyam (eat) banana'. You do not value
what is not yours: 'Black fowl no fe you, you call him John Crow'.
A man should not put himself in the power of his enemy: 'When
cockroach make dance him no ask fowl'. When a powerful man
falls even the feeblest can take advantage of him: 'When cotton tree
fall down, even nanny goat jump over him'. No one should over-
reach himself:

'One finger can't catch dog-flea';
'Dog have four foot but him can't walk four different ways';
'Hang your basket where you can reach it'.

It is wise to keep a guard on one's tongue:

'When you go to donkey house don't talk about ears';
'You catch cow by him horn but man by him word';
'De dog that carry bone come will carry bone go'.

The Yoruba proverb has more embroidery to it and is more con-
templative, but it makes the same kind of ironic comment on life. It
describes the leniency of a mother to her child:

'A mother will beat her child with a hollow hand'.

Another proverb warns a man not to over-estimate his power:

'The river carries away an elderly person who does not know his
weight',

and reminds us that no man can manage everything on his own:

'However sharp the knife, it cannot scratch its own handle'.

The West Indian proverb is more personal, sparkling with immediate appeal:

'You shake man's hand but you no' shake him heart'.

Take care to have means adequate for the job you undertake:

'You never see pop-gun kill alligator'.

Look after your own interests:

'You can't keep crow from flying but you can keep him from pitching on you' head'.

The entry of a third person puts an end to gossip:

'When six yeye (eyes) meet, story done'.

Beware how you mock at others:

'Little pig ask him mumma (mother) say what make her mout' so long; she say, "Never mind, me pickney; that same thing that make fe me (mine) long will make fe you long too".'

The Yoruba is tactful in pointing out the mistakes or faults of others, saying:

'Do not be seen counting the toes of a man who has only nine';

whereas the West Indian proverb accuses and censures. An insignificant man who is pompous and poor people who show off should remember that:

'Dog Mauger, (thin) him head big'; that is, it is the thin dog that has a big head.

A chit-chat should learn prudence from the cow:

'Not because cow don't have tongue, him don't talk'.

One who has not the means to live properly yet is always inviting guests should learn that:

'Hog never have water fe (to) wash but have it to give 'way'.

Both eyes are African, but they look at the world from different societies; the Yoruba and Ghanaian from a stable secure society in which throughout the centuries the elders have spoken and historical experience has shown that 'When we divide the meat, the gall must get its share'. The West Indian's experience is one in which some got all the gall. His proverbs are witty, but few are gay; his comment is ironic rather than happy, for with the sparkle, the keen sense of the comic, the inventiveness and the generosity there are sombre moods, inaccessible loneliness. The plantation taught that:

'Poor man never vex (because he dare not show his anger)';
'White man yeye (eyes) burn neger (Negro)';
'Not everybody who kin dem teet wid you is you fren.' (Not
everyone that smiles with you is your friend);
'Man you can't beat, you have fe call him fren';
'Every day you goad donkey, one day him will kick you';
'When black man t'ief (steals) him t'ief half-a-bit (five cents),
when backra (white man) t'ief him t'ief whole estate'.

Proverbs and 'old time sayings' are passing out but today use the
same language as yesterday. In the market-place and on the crowded
bus words and phrases of the same bright coinage are exchanged. A
man who sees a debtor passing by cries out that he sees some of his
money straying away down the street. In Lamming's novel, *The
Emigrants*, a friend tells the newly arrived emigrant Tornado, who
complains that the ground feels harder than at home, 'Yuh foot got
to get acclimatized. People don't go barefoot here, partner, so yuh
better tell yuh toes to make peace wid yer boots.' When Jamaica
became independent its leading exponent of folklore, Louise
Bennett, put the matter in the language of the ordinary people:

> *Independence wid a vengeance*
> *Independence raisin' Cain.*
> *Jamaica start grow beard, I hope*
> *We chin can stan' de strain.* . . .

The Trinidad calypso is gay and sparkling, but it often makes caustic
comments on life. The season for calypso is the 30 of the 40 days
before Lent. During this time rival Calypsonians sing in the 'tents'
where night after night crowds gather; rich, middle class and poor,
respectable church people and saga boys dressed in sheath-like saga
pants, 'peg top trousers' and saga coats called Bim-Bams, with wasp
waist and a vent in the back; East Indians, Negroes, French creole,
Syrians, Jews, Venezuelans crowd together, mothers of families and
'little numbers' or 'mopsies', professional men, workers from the oil
fields and cane fields and hangers on from the city. For the occasion
one community laughs at each salacious sally, at the singer's version

143

of some local or international scandal, at innuendo and detailed description, perhaps about a girl who

> had a face like a movie star
> And a figure like a car wid too much bumper . . .

But the calypso is much more than an item on an evening's programme. The expert uses it to pierce the rising folly as it flies to transfix social pretensions, to attack race and colour prejudice, to mock at the use of English schoolbooks not relevant to West Indian circumstances, to deride even the highest:

> What is love, mister? I do not know,
> But that it's powerful it was clearly shown,
> For it made a monarch give up his throne . . .

and
> In this world I know there are millions of whites
> Who appreciate the coloured man's rights,
> And has a desire and willingness
> To aid in his pursuit of happiness.
> A white man would love a Negro to the core
> As a brother, but not a brother-in-law. . . .

and they picture the desperation of men who come out of the terrible slums that once existed in John-John on the limits of Port-of-Spain:

> They can't see Chinese come from China
> They have big shop and grocery,
> Indians come from India
> Buying motor cars just like souvenir,
> Syrians come from Syria
> And own half the stores in town,
> And leave them so-called John-Johns
> To live with corbeaux in shanty town . . .

or the spread of unemployment:

> We were freed from slavery
> But still we in captivity,
> We have no food to eat
> But these big shots suppress our family.

As for differences of race, the Mighty Dougla, who is half East Indian, half Negro (hence the name 'dougla') considering the demand that all Africans should be sent to Africa, Indians to India, Syrians to Syria, commented:

> *You can send the Indians to India,*
> *And the Negroes back to Africa,*
> *But will somebody please tell me*
> *Where they sending me, poor me?*
> *I'm neither one nor the other,*
> *Six of one, half a dozen of the other,*
> *If they serious 'bout sending back people in true,*
> *They're going to have to split me in two. . . .*

Yet, this glittering form itself began as a protest. One of the finest calypsonians of the 1960s is correct when he describes the origin of calypso in *The Slave*:

> *We had to chant and sing*
> *To express our feelings,*
> *To that wicked and cruel man*
> *That was the only medicine*
> *To make him listen,*
> *And so Calypso began.*

The contrasts that are characteristic of the West Indies appear in the differences between the calypsos of Trinidad and the folk-songs of Jamaica. Some of these are linked with folk-games, including ring games which children play after school in country districts. Others are work songs, in which a leader sets the time and the group sings the chorus: as in the song Hill and Gully rider, for men working with picks. As they swing the hoe or pick above their shoulders the leader begins and the group sings the refrain:

> *Hill and gully rider,*
> *Hill and gully,*
> *If you tumble down you bruk you neck*
> *Hill and gully,*

145

> *If you bruk you neck you go to hell,*
> *Hill and gully,*
> *If you go to hell de debbil glad*
> *Hill and gully,*
> *Oh hill and gully rider,*
> *Hill an' gully.*

Other songs describe incidents in daily life, such as the return of a man from Panama, dressed in a fine new suit. He never learnt how to read a watch. Now he has a watch and a long chain – brass, not gold 'dah lick him belly, bam, bam, bam'; but if you ask him the time 'him look upon de sun'. A woman sitting all day in Linstead market before a basket full of ackees has waited in vain for a customer. She has not sold even three cents worth, 'a quattie wut'. Some took up the ackees in their hands, felt them and put them back in the basket. Now evening draws on and there is a hungry child waiting at home:

> *Carry me ackee go ah Linstead market,*
> *Not a quattie wut sell;*
> *Carry me ackee go ah Linstead market*
> *Not a quattie wut sell;*
> *Lard, what a night, not a bite,*
> *What a Saturday night.*
>
> *Everybody come feel up, feel up,*
> *Not a quattie wut sell,*
> *Everybody come feel up, feel up,*
> *Not a quattie wut sell.*

One of the loveliest of these songs is *Day dah light*. Women used to sing this while they carried bunches of bananas from the wharf into the hold of a waiting ship. Olivier described the scene:

> 'I watched them from above as they hurried to and from the iron-jawed hatches that gaped in the side of the ship, clear as day under the glare of the arc lights. The women came at a smooth noiseless double, the heavy head load poised, just steadied with a touch of the fingers, the face thrown a little forward, the chin raised, the

146

eyelids dropped to the level, intent, expressionless. . . . On each side of the doorways stood a Negro lad with a cutlass, the runners slackened pace as they passed him; if a stalk were too long at either end of the bunch, a flick of the blade and off it flew on the plank' ing. They were spotted and streaked now from the shoulder to the hem with dark stains of banana juice. The gowns hung in tat' tered fringes, disguising all human form, except where too full a bosom strained their holding'.[149]

At daybreak when the day grew light, the run slowed to a walk:

> *Day oh, day oh,*
> *Day dah light an' ah wan' fe go home,*
> *Day oh, day oh,*
> *Day dah light an' ah wan' fe go home. . . .*

The folk tales have, as their chief character a Spider, Anansi.[150] He travelled across the Atlantic with the wretched captives from Ashantiland, was 'shipmate' with them and with them made his home in the islands; weak, yet almost always the victor; seeking always his own benefit yet somehow keeping the affection of Kisander the Cat, Moos'Moos, Dog, Parrot, Old Owl, Tumblebug, Sister Hen, even of Tiger, his chief adversary, and Jackass whom he tricked so shamefully. The stories should not be told while the sun is in the sky. They belong to evening'time. Then the Spider comes into the centre of a small circle of men and women sitting out in the open, talking and laughing together. As the old man tells the tale each listener adds his comment: 'Yes, dat clever man'; 'What a wicked Anansi'; 'Ah, dat old rogue, but him clever so!' The scent of night jasmine is in the air, of orange blossoms from the field near by, of earth newly ploughed, of the cow'pen. A bull'frog gurgles from the pond where cattle drink, tree'frogs and crickets make music which no one hears because they have always heard it. The circle draws a little closer for there are other people about; in Jamaica and Antigua, duppies; in Trinidad, jumbies, and the harmless dwen, a child who died un' christened before reaching the age of nine months; and terrible presences like diablesse, who slays men, taking them into the heart of the forest where they become 'dote', bemused; and seekuyans and legawas who shed their skins and suck the blood of men and animals, like the one that they saw in Grenada at about five o'clock in the morning, when the donkey in the stable panicked and they caught sight of a naked creature trying to get at the animal, and at the sign of the cross it vanished into the air. Anansi's world has none of these terrors. Laughter follows him as he sets out to trick Jackass:

'Once upon a time and a long time ago, Anansi was sitting out in the yard at evening-time. Cool breeze was blowing from the hill and Anansi say to himself, "Dats Christmas breeze"; and a drum begin to beat and a flute begin to play and Anansi say, "Dat's Christmas music, dat's Christmas John Canoe. But what about de prize Busha is giving for the best dancer dis Christmas?"

'So Anansi begin to work him head. He pull out his purse. No money in it. He go into the house and pull out the trunk under the bed and look under the clothes. No money. "I better win dat prize," Anansi say to himself.

'Anansi start to study his head again. Busha promise to give a prize for the best dance in the John Canoe masquerade. He take up a piece of sugar-cane and break it and eat it; then another piece and break it and eat it. Anansi go on working his head and chewing the sugar-can till on a sudden him feel lively. Hear him to himself: "Stop, dat cane juice strong, me head feel light, me foot feel light", and he dance and jump into the air and dance again until at last he fall down. He say: "If I dance like this at the John Canoe I must win the prize." Then Anansi was quiet for half an hour, working his brain till he said, "Dat cane juice strong; if it goes to my foot I will cut figure and win, but if it goes to my head I would get fool-fool."

'Next morning Anansi went into the cane field and cut cane fast fast, and squeezed the juice into a large pan. He picked it up and went off singing. By and by Anansi stopped by the side of the river to talk to Mother Hen who was washing her clothes, and he stopped by the shop to talk to Mr Parrot and he stopped near the field by the school to talk to Brother Bull, and everywhere he said

148

"Happy Christmas, Happy Christmas, I hope to see you to-morrow at the John Canoe", and each one asked "What costume will you dress in, Anansi?" To each one he said, "Me, I won't wear any costume at all, but I will win the prize!" After he went off Brother Bull burst out laughing and said "Stupid Fellow. He must be getting old. Who ever heard of anyone going to John Canoe without dressing up?"

'Anansi went along, whistling till he got to the yard where Mr Jackass lived and he saw Jackass drinking water out of a pan. He said: "Mr Jackass, can you give me some water?" "Why Anansi take it if you want it." Jackass was a very rude man, very sudden in his speech. Anansi said "T'ank you, Jackass, t'ank you for true." When he tasted the water he made up his face, spat it out, and said "Oh Brother Jackass, what bad water. Mine is sweeter."

"'Where you keep you' water?" asked Jackass.

"'I just have a little in this shut-pan," said Anansi, "but you can take a taste."

'Anansi held the pan and Jackass took a big mouthful. "Shame on you, Mr Jackass, what a big taste you take, man!"

"'But it's sweet, give me some more; it's good water." Anansi replied, "Sorry Mr Jackass, I can't give you more now; but I tell you what. In the morning I bring more for you, and then we go off to the John Canoe together." Jackass said, "Oh no, I don't mix up myself wid all those people at the John Canoe."

'Anansi smiled and said, "Ah well, we will see, we will see, Mr Jackass."

'Next morning Anansi got up early and went into the cane field. He took a demijohn with him and filled it with the cane juice. Then he set out for the yard where Jackass lived. Jackass was on the look out for him. He ran to meet Anansi, took the demijohn from him, and drank and drank the cane juice till none was left. Then the cane juice went to his head and he flung away the demijohn and began to laugh and jump and dance. Anansi jumped on his back and held his ears, and rode him out into the road at the very time when the John Canoe dancers came by, and Anansi joined the procession.

'Now Anansi was at the head of the procession, and everybody was dancing, Hen, Sister Cow, Brother Bull, Parrot and Kisander the Cat and everybody was dressed in costume.

'Anansi whispered in Jackass' ear, "Brother Jackass, cut figure man, dance man, dance!"

'Jackass started to jump and prance and flash his tail.

'Anansi whispered again: "Open you' mouth, Jackass, and show you teeth and dance, man dance!"

'Jackass showed his teeth and worked his jawbone up and down.

'Anansi whispered in his ears: "Wiggle-wiggle you ears, man, and dance, Jackass, dance!"

'Jackass wiggled his ears and danced. Every time he slowed down Anansi told him what to do, to turn round and round, to stand on his two back feet, to dance with his head down and his tail up, until everybody else stopped dancing and watched Jackass. Poor Jackass jumped and pranced and danced till he danced the cane juice out of himself and dropped to the ground and fell asleep with tiredness.

'Anansi jumped off his back and called out: "I demand the grand prize me and my Jackass." The whole crowd shouted: "You win it, you and your Jackass." Busha gave him the prize, and said that every year there must always be a Jackass to dance and cut figure in the John Canoe.

'But poor Jackass was too ashamed after that. He would never go the John Canoe, so every year somebody dresses up like Ass-head and jump John Canoe. That's how Ass-head get into John Canoe; and that's why Jackass always looks like him sorry for himself. Is Anansi cause it all to happen.

'Jack Mandora, I don't choose none.'

As in the proverbs and songs, the dance and music the people created in these stories their own separate world of entertainment which belonged to the yard and hut, not to 'Big Massa' in the large house on the hill. Here, as in the sayings, greed, envy and vanity were ridiculed. And was there not a deeper satisfaction in a world where strength did not always carry the day nor power win the final victory?

The stories and proverbs are static; but folk music is vigorous and popular, extending its influence throughout the whole community in the calypsos and the revivalist songs of Jamaica and, through the steelband, which was first developed in the years immediately following the end of the last war. The story is an extraordinary one, how poor men, some with little education, invented new musical instruments out of empty oil drums and developed a characteristic music which it would be very difficult to reduce to writing; with subtle half-notes and shades of tone 'reminiscent of but not quite the same as the flattened fifth of American jazz' and with 'a certain off-colour that is peculiarly intriguing to the Western-trained ear'.

The story begins early in the nineteenth century in Trinidad with 'bands' formed by African slaves in districts settled by French planters, 'convois' or 'regiments' with high sounding names, Dreadnaught Band, Danish Regiment, Monkey Corps and the like.[151] The tradition of the band[152] is strong in the Carnival of present-day Trinidad, but it was interrupted by the Second World War. They included men who 'beat bamboo' that is, pieces of bamboo of different lengths that were used as drums. One of the bandsmen discovered that by bending a length of reinforcing steel and hanging it triangle-wise from his thumb he could beat out a tune. From this the bands progressed to beating empty tins hung around the neck, or lengths of metal. The next discovery was that if one hammered the bottom of an empty paint can from within, the bumps and hollows gave out sounds of different notes. Triumph followed in the late 1940s when one of the bands, Bar-20, used sawed-off pans with drum-sticks to get their famous 'cut and tumble' beat; and when another 'panman' wrapped his drumsticks with strips of rubber, cut off the top of an oil-drum at a length of about 8 inches, marked or 'seamed' the pan with a number of radii, all at the same distance from the circumference. He found a way of tuning the drum by using heat and tapping the different 'notes'. In this way the first steel drum band was created. The instruments of the present-day steel-band include the Booms, three, four or even six full-sized empty 40-gallon oil drums, cut off at the bottom, with the tops stretched by beating into a convex shape. The 'notes' are then marked off or 'seamed' with a hammer and cold chisel. After this the pan is burned, and at the right moment oil is thrown on to it. This tempers the steel. The tuning follows. This is an intricate matter, calling for a true ear and for great patience and skill in the use of the tuning instruments, a small tinker's hammer and a 2-lb sledge. The Cello pan is shorter than the Boom. It has five or six notes to the three or four of the Boom. Also, there are Guitar pans that have 14 notes, and the Ping-pong, a steel drum cut 6 inches from the top, stretched and tempered, and marked with 26 or 32 notes.

These art-forms and customs belong to a black world to which 70 out of every 100 West Indians have belonged for most of their history.[153] Since they had no money with which to hire labour, they pooled their strength and worked for each other in an exchange labour system: the 'combite' of Haiti, the 'lift system' of the Leeward Islands, or a 'jollification' in which a man who wanted some work done invited his friends and neighbours and provided a hot meal and rum, but made no other payment. In Curacao the people 'worked simadan' and sang 'guenee' a language full of African words. In Jamaica they had a 'day for day' or a 'lend day' and in Trinidad a 'gaiapa', the men of some remote village working together to clear and plant the land while the women prepared a meal of yams, cush-cush and plantain, with pickled meat, salted cod fish (in Trinidad with agouti as well), and some deer. They formed 'partnerships' and 'susu', known as 'Esusu' among the Yorubas of Nigeria, in order to provide themselves with savings. In a 'susu' several persons club together and subscribe every week an agreed sum. The jackpot is paid over to members in turn. Much more highly organized, and now a permanent part of West Indian life are the Friendly or Benevolent Societies and the Burial Scheme Society, in which numbers of persons join together to provide a form of sick benefit and funeral insurance.

The parades and the anniversaries of these organizations with their uniforms and robes gave the glitter of ceremony that added meaning to six days spent in the banana and cane fields. The ranks and titles provided opportunity for leadership and social standing. What mattered most to a man was his respect, the acknowledgment of himself as a person. The bitterest insult was to make him feel ashamed in public, to strip him of covering, to 'expose' him, or 'shame' him. The West Indian poet D. Walcott, in his moving play, *The Sea at Dauphin*, which owes much to the Irish poet J. M. Synge, with unerring instinct put into the mouth of an old man the words:

'Look, give me my respect you hear. I know you since you been wetting this same pants you have, piece of the canot is yours but give me my respect or we mashing up now self.'

But the major institutions were not those that originated with the people. The Church, Christian marriage, the secondary school, even the police court belonged to a white or brown world. If you were white or middle-class brown the law was the guardian of liberty; if you were poor it might be the instrument of extortion, the means by which one who had training and could 'handle language' got hold of the property of a poor man who had not paid his rent.

Yet the ordinary people discovered their land many generations ahead of the West Indian intellectual. They worked the land, and learned that the peacock hides its ugly legs when someone praises the startling beauty of its tail, that a cock cannot ride a horse though it has a spur, nor the hog get fat until the guavas ripen. They knew their own pocket-handkerchief field as 'fe me piece of ground'. They marked the years by events, when 'Governor Richards come' or the 'Hurricane blow'. They judged men quickly and without error, by whether 'their spirit take to them' or not, discerning in a moment that the new overseer on the property was 'bad minded', the shopkeeper covetous or 'cubbitch', the new teacher conceited or 'consequential'. They learned that the great moments of life were birth and death and that one can tell from the clots of blood or knots in the umbilical cord how many children a woman is destined to bear; and that when a boy comes to manship he should build a house, even only with one room, for 'if crab don't have hole him never get fat'. The goals in life are clearly defined. To have 10 acres of mountain land is wealth. A man is able 'to manage' on 2 acres, but he must go off to the sugar estate to 'look work' at crop time. At 25 a man should have achieved a certain standing, at 40 what is appropriate to that age.

Life is never easy for these people nor a man completely secure. Those who became involved in law suits found it wise not only to hire a lawyer but also to employ a 'four-eye man' who by magic could gain the verdict. If one were ill there were balm yards and powerful baths made up of herbs picked and prepared by a wise woman.[154] To cure swollen feet one could hold the front feet of a frog with one hand, the back feet with another and rub the body of the frog on the swollen foot. Then tie the frog securely and hang it in a tree. When the frog dies the swelling goes down. With leaves and plants one could deal with fever, boils, dysentery, cuts, and even 'maljo', the strange fever a child gets when a person with a 'bad eye' looks at him. If one's woman is 'running around' there are charms that will keep her tied to her man. A girl can do the same with her 'wild man'. And for a love charm to keep a man or a woman mix together the gizzard of a chicken, wild okra seeds, lamp powder, grated nutmeg, black pepper, attar of roses powder, and sprinkle a small amount on the food of the person in question.

This world of the peasant and working-class man was ignored or despised by the educated West Indian just as it was ignored in Haiti by the Haitian intellectual until Jean Price Mars called on Haitian scholars 'to seek around them their sources of inspiration, in the mores, character studies and social attitudes which determine our manner of loving, of hating, of believing – our manner of life'. Later Morisseau LeRoy wrote:[155]

I am remaking my garden
May the weeds grow no more,
May the sun burn it no more

I am reconstructing my temple
O my nights O my moons
I am rebuilding my temple
May men respect it
May the gods respect it.

12   West Indian Themes

ROOTED IN HIS HOLDING and village, the peasant spoke
through his folksongs and stories. He handed these down from
generation to generation by word of mouth. But the West Indian
intellectual remained silent. There was no West Indian literature
before the 1930s. Not until the early 1940s did the West Indian
novel emerge. Craftsmen made fine furniture in the style of Chippen-
dale and Sheraton but there were no West Indian sculptors. Women
plaited intricate patterns in straw and fibre but there were no West
Indian painters. Revivalists danced when the Power took possession
of them and children in their ring games translated music into gesture
and movement, but there were no West Indian dance groups, no
choreographers. The countryman's comment on life in his proverbs
had no counterpart in written literature. This was in contrast with
Latin America and Cuba and Haiti where there was a literary
tradition, and where an important part in the struggle for independence and the spread of revolutionary ideas was taken by the
'pensador'. In this tradition were leaders like de Miranda of Venezuela, of whom Napoleon said that he had a sacred fire in his soul,
and Jose Marti, who built up the independence movement in Cuba
with his burning pen.

Two forces brought about a change in the islands. One was the
growth of national sentiment, the other the discovery of the West
Indies by intellectuals studying in the capitals of the metropolitan
powers during the years following the First World War at a time
when many European intellectuals became leaders in the socialist
movement. The colonial revolutions that destroyed the empire began
in Oxford, London and the Sorbonne. Indian, West African and

West Indian intellectuals were involved. Later the socialist philo-sophy became a moving force with West Indian political leaders like Adams, Manley, Nethersole and Errol Barrow. But the change in interest and in attachment extended beyond politics, manifesting itself in almost every aspect of West Indian life. In the case of Eric Williams it revealed itself first in the field of scholarship, for it was at a much later date that he entered politics. His brilliant study *Capitalism and Slavery* threw new light on the abolition of the British slave trade and the emancipation of slaves in the British Empire by establishing the fact that new forces generated by the industrial revo-lution and hostile to the old mercantile system were primarily respon-sible. Williams followed up this study with a later work, *The Negro in the Caribbean*, in which he praised the West Indian working-class movement that emerged in the 1930s and appealed to the middle classes to join the masses in freeing the islands from colonialism.

There was another pioneer historical study of this period that reinforced the theme, *The Black Jacobins*, a powerful penetrating work on the Haitian Revolution, by C. L. R. James. He pointed out that the British discovered the value of free trade through the American Revolution and the break-away of the colonies.

'But if Britain gained, the British West Indies suffered. The rising industrial bourgeoisie feeling its way to free trade and a greater exploitation of India began to abuse the West Indies, called them "sterile rocks" and asked if the interest and independence of the nation should be sacrificed to 72,000 masters and 400,000 slaves'?[156]

These three books gave to the West Indian a historical reason for rejecting colonial attitudes, and encouraged him to make new assess-ments of himself and his role in history. Traditionally the educated West Indian had ignored the darker side of his heritage in favour of the lighter. He had taught himself to black-out a part of the real world. Current ideas about the West Indies had been fashioned and shaped in England and in France to suit the intellectual needs of these countries and to satisfy deep political and religious motivations.[157]

Now, a century after emancipation, the West Indian intellectual and politician began to set himself free by looking at his origins and by identifying himself with the West Indies.

For some West Indian intellectuals this meant a search for roots, for an indigenous element such as that which the Mexican or Bolivian nationalist finds in his American Indian heritage. In that search for cultural continuity Haya de la Torre of Peru claimed that 'the Indian subconscious lives in us all'. This has no meaning for the islands. Where the Latin-American intellectual became Indianist the Cuban and Haitian became African, and the way to this new assessment of, and pride in, Africa was opened up by West Indians. James has pointed out that the role of Africa in the consciousness of the West Indian people proved itself to be a stage in the West Indian quest for a national identity.

'Today the emancipation of Africa is one of the outstanding events of contemporary history. Between the wars when this emancipation was being prepared, the unquestioned leaders of the movement in every public sphere, in Africa itself, in Europe and in the United States, were not Africans but West Indians.'[158]

Two of the leading names in this movement were Marcus Garvey, to whom reference has already been made, and George Padmore, who founded the African Bureau, the only African organization of its kind between the wars. Of the seven members of the Committee five were West Indians.

In the Caribbean, Africa became a word of power,[159] especially at the popular level. Garvey proved this and the Ras Tafari also. The Cuban scholar Ortiz sought through his work to provide a basis for Afro-Cubanism. The writings of Luis Pales Matos of Puerto Rico, whose *Tuntun de Pasa y Grafería* was reprinted in that island in 1950, have as a basic theme the fact that Puerto Rico, is one-half Spanish and the other half African. The poet is 'obsessed by the remote Vision of a Negro people'. In Haiti, in 1928, Jean Price Mars started a new movement among young Haitian writers with his *Ainsi Parla l'Oncle*, in which he examined the African heritage of the Haitian,

knowing full well 'the wall of repugnance against which I am striking by daring to speak to you of Africa and African things'. Another
Haitian poet, Jacques Roumain, in *Bois d'Ebene*, expressed his agony
over the Middle Passage and the cheapness of Negro life, of pieces of
ebony wood, bits of ivory. Looking back he declared: 'I have kept
your memory, Africa, you are in me'. No less passionate is Aimé
Césaires memorable poem, *Cahier d'un Retour au Pays Natal*, published in Paris in 1939 in which he contrasted the 'white world its
horrible exhaustion from its immense labours' with his negritude
which

> *. . . is no tower, no cathedral,*
> *It cleaves into the red flesh of the teeming earth*
> *It cleaves into the glowing flesh of the heavens. . . .*[160]

Respect for Africa was essential if the man of the Caribbean was to
have any respect for himself. In this sense the statement of James is
fair:

> 'The West Indians were and had always been Western-educated.
> West Indian society confined black men to a very narrow strip of
> social territory. The first step to freedom was to go abroad. Before
> they could begin to see themselves as free and independent people
> they had to clear from their minds the stigma that anything African
> was inherently inferior and degraded. The road to West Indian
> national identity lay through Africa.'[161]

This applies to all the islands save Trinidad, where the chief problem is that of generating a sense of national unity between those whose
road lies through Africa and those whose road leads from India.

The dominant themes in West Indian literature are race and colour
rather than Africa and Negritude. Reference has already been made
to questions of colour and class in the West Indies, and to that self-
depreciation, even self-hatred, which a gifted young West Indian
Negro, a social scientist, described:

> 'A black young woman who destroys a photographic print of
> herself because it is printed too black; and an older black woman

who indicates that she is giving her vote to a white candidate since no black man can help me in this country these days. The examples just quoted are based on actual occurrences and betray an interesting ambivalence on the part of these people in their attitudes to race.'[162]

The conflict is further expressed in an illuminating poem by a sophisticated brown West Indian:[163]

> Ancestor on the auction block
> Across the years your eyes seek mine
> Compelling me to look.
> I see your shackled feet
> Your sensitive black face
> I see your humiliation
> And turn away
> Ashamed.
>
> Across the years your eyes seek mine
> Compelling me to look.
> Is this mean creature that I see
> Myself?
> Ashamed to look
> Because of myself ashamed
> Shackled by my own ignorance
> A slave.
>
> Humiliated
> I cry to the eternal abyss
> For understanding.
> Ancestor on the auction block
> Across the years your eyes meet mine,
> Electric
> I am transformed.

No reference is made to the other ancestor who stood by the side of the auction block ready to make his purchases, whereas in Guillen's *Ballad of My Two Grandfathers*[164] both African and European appear:

> *Lance with head of bone*
> *Drum of leather and wood:*
> *My black grandfather.*
> *Ruff round his broad throat*
> *Grey warrior's armour:*
> *My white grandfather . . .*

In him they both meet,

> *I bring them together. . . .*
> *Black anguish and white anguish*
> *Both of the same stature.*
> *And they shout. And dream. And weep. And sing.*
> *And sing – and sing – and sing.*

The novelist Mittelholzer, in his novel *Morning at the Office*, depicted the secret corrosive influence of colour in the individualistic society of Trinidad, the correlation between whiteness and class structure, the bitterness within a brown man who resents the attitudes of white people and yet is compelled to ally himself with them rather than with black people, the inner conflicts in a man who feels himself unable to fulfil his capacities because of his colour.

The conflict may become collision, as in the dramatic scene in Hearne's novel,[165] *Land of the Living*, in which one of the Ras Tafari, symbolizing not the reality but the myth of Africa as a living faith confronts a group of coloured middle-class West Indian students:

'He stood there as I came up; a tall still figure, not simply thin but lean as a strayed domestic animal becomes gaunt and harsh on its own foraging. A tremendous tensed hardness seemed to radiate from that narrow body . . .

'"Well now," he said with an impersonal waggish derision more corrosive than hate, "W'at a t'ing I see today. Is not only de brown man run from de black, de white man run too." From far back in the rough forest of shaggy beard, matted hair and heavy writhing brows, his eyes glared with a bleak unwinding ferocity in which we were not even reflected, as if we were the brute, anonymous means by which he contemplated ideals of hostility beyond our scope. "Yuh t'ink say I was gwuine fe steal you car?" . . .

"'An' I know say how de white man eat up de children of Africa an' hold dem in bondage." He began to shake, and his angry shining gaze grew dull and blind; and his voice took on a throbbing exalted note: "Dis land an' de whole eart' belong to de white man, an' de black is his slave. You come here fe make more plot against we black. But our day is come. Our God will come; black and shining and terrible . . . Africa's children will turn and rule . . ." He was swaying now in a series of abrupt convulsions, his voice hoarse. He seemed to claw dazedly for words in the air . . . "Africa will rule and de children of Africa will be as princes over all on dat day . . . All nation shall bow down to Africa an' to de Emperor of Ethiopia an' his people . . ."'

West Indian writers who have established a reputation in the international world of letters include the novelists Lamming, Naipaul, Hearne, Mittelholzer, Selvon, Salkey, Vic Reid, and the poets Walcott, Hendriks, Seymour. Most of these give a central place to the African peasant in the Caribbean, departing in the process from the accustomed path to security through conformity with social values based on pigmentation and race. At times the mood is that of protest at past wrongs and present frustrations, as in the lines of Roach:[166]

> All the tales come mocking me
> Out of the slave plantations where I grubbed
> Yam and cane; where heat and hate sprawled down
> Among the cane – my sister sired without
> Love or law . . .

but rarely is the note as passionately angry as in Luis Pales Matos picture of his green Antillean island, Puerto Rico:

> *This is my whole history:*
> *Salt, sterility, weariness . . .*
> *a cry out of the depths.*

He appeals to God to have pity on his poor town where 'my poor people will die from nothing'. As despairing are the lines of Sylvain of Haiti:[167]

> *My despairing soul sings despair.*
> *Keep away from the black midnight . . .*
> *I am sad tonight*
> *The vast sadness*
> *Of a murdered race . . .*

The novelists are more passionate and intense than the poets. Two have turned to the West Indian past. One is Vic Reid[168] who, in *New Day*, describes a rising of peasants at Morant Bay in Jamaica in 1865, when a protest against the injustice of the local magistracy and against the attitude of the government ended in beatings and the gallows. Reid then switched from the defeat of 1865 to the triumph of the peasant in 1944 when responsible government was introduced into Jamaica.

The other novelist who turned to West Indian history was Mitteholzer.[169] In his Kaywana novels he pictured the turbulent past of Guyana, the hostility of estate owner and slave, of white and black, and the mulatto caught midway in the swift current of hatred, all in an atmosphere of almost intolerable violence and sadism.

Most West Indian novelists, however, are concerned with the present. As Lamming pointed out[170] in *Pleasures of Exile*, in the 1940s the West Indian discovered the novel as a way of 'investigating and projecting the inner experiences of the West Indian community'. Selvon,[171] for example, painted vivid pictures of peasant and lower middle-class life in the villages of Trinidad and in Port-of-Spain, writing with a quick natural wit and a sense of the comic in an idiom that is essentially Trinidadian. In *Brighter Sun* he tells how:

'In Trinidad there is a short cut to identity. All Americans for instance are known as "Joes". East Indians are hailed as "Ram" or

"Singh" or some other common name until an association is formed and introductions made. Though this method of identi/ fying unknowns is not used among the middle or upper class, it is the custom of the working class to address strangers in this manner. In the same way all Chinese are "Chins". Not that it matters a great deal with the Chinaman as long as his shop or laundry is well patronized. But if it happens that he takes unto himself a Creole wife she demands that he be addressed properly. . . .

'In Barataria they began to call Tall Boy that from the very first, because he was tall and young . . . He moved into Barataria with a pregnant wife and four little boys with scarcely a year between each of them. Mary was doomed to be always with child when she married Tall Boy but she was Chinese and she accepted it. When the women in the village got to know her well, they said "Is how dis' Tall Boy running yuh down so? He must be full of blood."'

It is with this lower middle/class world that writers like Naipaul,[172] Lamming and Mais deal. The treatment is differentiated by the personality of the writer and of the island society of which he is a part. Nowhere is the difference between Trinidad and Barbados more clearly seen than in the works of the East Indian Naipaul and the West Indian Negro Lamming. Each has known the deadly frus/ trations that Lamming described in an early short story, *Birds of a Feather*, the hateful business of conformity to lower middle/class life, the isolation of the individual, the way in which poverty destroyed men and women. In his first novel, *In the Castle of My Skin*, he described an island society that was almost wholly Victorian:

'the High School which was intended to educate the children of the clerical and professional classes, the village school that served the needs of the villagers who were poor, simple and without a very marked sense of social prestige'.

This was a kind of society contemporaneous with Trollope and Dickens but with the added complication of colour.

Lamming's world is West Indian Negro, Naipaul's East Indian

Trinidadian, the old Hindu values existing in the middle of a creole world to which the East Indian also belongs. In a brilliant novel *A House for Mr Biswas*, Naipaul shows how a Mr Mohun Biswas devoted a lifetime to securing a house, his own place, something that was unquestionably his own. But the opening words of the prologue are 'Ten weeks before he died, Mr Mohun Biswas a journalist of Sikkim Street, St James, Port-of-Spain, was sacked. . . .' This is the verdict on a life yet to be lived, the end of a story yet to be told.

Less sophisticated but more savage is the symbolism of Orlando Patterson,[173] a West Indian of the generation following Naipaul and Lamming, who, in his novel, *Children of Sisyphus*, portrays the Dungle, a part of the slums in West Kingston where in past times the garbage of the city was dumped, and where in present times Jamaica has dumped its poor. Throughout the book human effort is represented in terms of garbage. The story begins with a man driving a garbage cart to the dump, his stick sucking the life out of his dying mule. At the end, the garbage man collects the bleeding body of one of the chief characters, a prostitute named Dinah who tried to climb out of the 'garbage society' in which she was born.

The themes of race, colour and of the personal necessity for achieving some measure of inner security recur throughout West Indian literature. The novelist is concerned with more than investigating and projecting the West Indian experience. He personally is involved, and so his work is marked by a strong social consciousness, an acute concern that flows from a discovery of identity. This is clear in the novels of Roger Mais, in which the harsh circumstances of life in the slums of West Kingston are treated with knowledge and with a moving tenderness for men and women; in the natural insight and directness of Selvon in stories such as *The Lonely Londoners*; and in Naipaul who at first sight seems to stand apart from the West Indian world and its people. He describes their way of life with a keen eye for the ludicrous and a pervasive irony, his laughter at times becoming mockery, as in the account of the dinner at Government House to which newly elected Members of the Legislative Council were invited. The wife of Ganesh Ramsumair 'couldn't bear the thought of eating off other peoples plates. It was like going to a restaurant. You don't know what the food are and you don't know who cook it.' The new member for one of the Port-of-Spain wards turned up in a khaki suit with sun helmet; the blackest member of the Legislative Council wore a three-piece blue suit, yellow woollen gloves and a monocle; an elderly Christian Indian member didn't bring a wife because he said he never had one, instead he brought along a daughter, a bright little thing of about four; Mrs Primrose, a wife of the blackest MLC explained that the other Mrs Primrose who the governor's wife had formerly met 'ain't the same me. The other one, the one you did see at the Mothers Union at Granadina, she at home. Making baby'.

Towards the end of dinner the man with the open shirt began to wonder 'how much car expenses they go pay we for coming here. I an't ask to dine with the Governor, you know. . . . The man with jodhpurs said 'But they got to pay we, man'.

This mockery is not characteristic of the novels, but it is directly in the mood of many of the Trinidad calypsos.

In contrast there is the scene in Lamming's novel, *In the Castle of My Skin*, where Boy Blue goes crabbing along the Barbados beach, thinking himself a master in the art of evading the rushing waves.

'A wave wrenched him and now he was actually in the sea. We shivered, dumb. A wave pushed him up and another completing the somersault plunged him down. He screamed and we screamed too. We screamed and the fisherman came out from behind the lighthouse. We motioned him to the spot where we had last seen Boy Blue. There was a faint scream in the air. We could not understand how it had happened. We could not follow the speed of the fisherman's movement. He had gathered up the net and tossed it in the sea over the area we had indicated. He hauled earnestly and the body of the net emerged with the strangest of all catches. Boy Blue was there. He was rolled up like a wet blanket. We were dumb with fright. He looked so impotent in the net as if it contained a useless dead thing. The fisherman looked at Boy Blue with a kind of disgust. . . . We were afraid of the fisherman.

The way he looked at us. He was like someone who had been sorry for what he did, and yet not sorry since he knew it had to be done. . . . He knew the catch was not a fish, but he hauled the net with the earnestness that could only have meant a desire beyond his control for the other's survival. Now he looked so terribly penitent. We were frightened.

'"I should have let you drown," he snarled, and his voice held terror.

'"Thank you, sir," said Boy Blue, catching his breath. It was the first time Boy Blue had spoken.

'"By Christ you should have drown," the fisherman snarled again.'

The boys strolled back to the village knowing that the man who had seemed so strong and remote, a giant, with absolute command of the waves and of his net, was not a giant but a man. 'Contact had made him human.'

Contact between the West Indian writer and his world of black and brown peasants and lower middle-class people resulted in a deep concern which is expressed in the West Indian novel often with the peasant's earthy, almost brutal realism, but rarely if ever with the self-defeating despair of Luis Pales Matos who writes of his island as being in the desert of a continent, 'bleating like a stewed goat'.

The emergence of the intellectual as a West Indian, as writer, scholar, politician provided the West Indies with a man who was able to formulate ideas from the local point of view. Up to the end of Crown Colony rule and for some years beyond that time ideas had flowed from the ruling class. The official or dominant themes were those of the metropolitan power they represented and of which they were a part. The ideas and values of this group still remain important and the political revolution that has taken place in the West Indies will only become fully effective when the intellectual takes over within his own society the important role of interpreting and transmitting ideas, of expressing in West Indian terms the symbols, images and themes that enlarge personal dignity and establish a people's role.

It is significant that in his attack on racial and colour discrimination the West Indian writer has not advocated racialism. In exposing
the destructive effects of colonialism and in strengthening national
feeling he has not rejected the concept of inter-dependence. . . . As
far as attitudes to race are concerned he echoes the words of Marti,[174]
that white and black racialists have no justification for complaining
about each other, because

'differential rights, contrary to nature, are the enemies of peace. The
white man who isolates himself also isolates the black man. The
black man who isolates himself isolates and provokes the white
man. . . . Man is more than white, mulatto, black.'

The West Indian writer, the lower middle-class man and the peasant
struggle for a world in which one set of people do not have to work
twice as hard in order to compete with another group. This is hardest
for the Negro, who, has a handicap of being years at the base of the
social pyramid. Psychologically he does not possess too strong a racial
memory of great cultural achievements as these European, Chinese
and Indian compatriots.

There is no strong anti-English or anti-American feeling reflected
in West Indian literature. One of the best of all West Indian poets,
Claude MacKay, almost a solitary voice in the 1920s, recognized the
greatness of the United States, which has given a home to thousands
of West Indians, and the terror of racial discrimination and the Klu
Klux Klan:

Although she feeds me bread of bitterness
And sinks into my throat her tiger's tooth
Stealing my breath of life, I will confess
I love this cultured hell that tests my youth. . . .
Her vigour flows like tides into my blood,
Giving me strength erect against her hate. . . .
Darkly I gaze into the days ahead
And see her might and granite wonders there,
Beneath the touch of times unerring hand,
Like priceless treasures sinking in the sand.

If MacKay had written about England in this poem he would probably have pictured the degradation of the slave plantation as well as respect and affection for England as the country that gave him his system of law, parliamentary government, his books and schools. The West Indian writer, like the West Indian governments and people, turns naturally to those countries and peoples with whom for three centuries he has been linked: North America, the United Kingdom and West Africa. He sees them as bound on the same voyage of exploration as himself, one that leads through an archi-pelago in which mankind dwells on islands separated by pressing tides of race and colour;[175] and he asks whether the voyage will lead to the discovery 'that no man is an island, entire of itself, but a piece of the continent, a part of the main'.

58 Carnival and festivity are part of West Indian folklore and custom. Christmas mummers in Jamaica 'playing John Canoe'.

59 Carnival time at Port-of-Spain, Trinidad. The Trinidad Carnival has its roots in the late eighteenth and early nineteenth centuries, in the 'bands' or 'convois' of the slaves.

60 (*left above*) Cricket, a 'national' sport which boasts names like Worrell, Headley, Constantine, Sobers, and 'Ramadin and Valentine'.

61 (*left below*) The steel band is entirely a West Indian achievement. The most famous 'steel bands' are those of Trinidad and Antigua.

62 The calypso, a form of Trinidadian folk music that has spread to the other islands.

63 Edna Manley is a West Indian sculptor who has gained an international reputation.

64 (*left above*) The large Anglican cathedrals are relics of the symbols of planter power and the established order. The cathedral in St John's Antigua was built during the nineteenth century.

65 Many of the East Indians of Trinidad have preserved their religious heritage. There are many mosques like this one in Trinidad.

66 In the West Indies there are many 'revivalist' sects, each with its own elaborate ritual and strong emotional appeal.

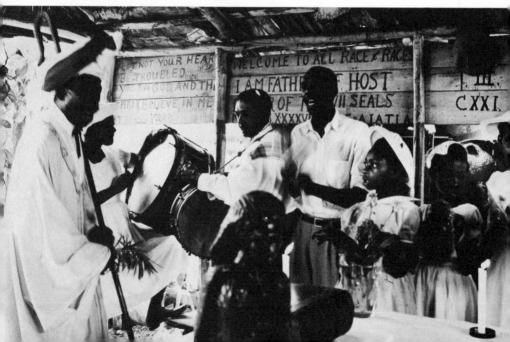

67 (*left above*) In the islands where French rule predominated, Roman Catholicism is strong. Many churches were built, like this one in Trinidad.

68 (*right above*) A Hindu temple in Trinidad.

69 In the West Indies there are a number of revivalist evangelical sects. This meeting place of the Assembly of God is in a Maroon township in Jamaica.

70 One of the objectives of the new West Indian governments is education for everyone. This primary school is at St Vincent in the Windward Islands.

71 The system of education follows the English pattern. This is at Knox College, a co-educational secondary school, in Jamaica.

72 The University of the West Indies admitted its first 33 students in 1948, and by 1966 it had 3,100. This is the administrative block at Mona in Jamaica. A second Campus was established in Trinidad in 1960, a third in Barbados in 1964.

73 The influence of the British educational system has even extended to the school uniform. This is at Roseau, Dominica.

74 As in many nations achieving independence there is marked evidence of affluence and there are problems of poverty. This is the Hilton Hotel at Port-of-Spain, Trinidad.

75 Shanty towns are being replaced by government-financed housing estates such as this one at Trench Town, Jamaica.

Notes on the Text

I THE WEST INDIAN EXPERIENCE

1 D. Lowenthal in *The Range and Variation of Caribbean Societies*, Annals of the New York Academy of Sciences, vol 83, pp 786–95, points out that 'a man who says "I am a Jamaican" or "I am a Barbadian" is very likely expressing the broadest allegiance he knows'.

2 J. A. Froude, *The English in the West Indies*, London, 1888.

3 G. Freyre, *The Masters and the Slaves*, New York, 1946.

4 With reference to black, brown and white people in the Caribbean, P. Blanshard in *Democracy and Empire in the Caribbean* observes that the islands, with the exception of Puerto Rico, are racially more African and East Indian than European—and everywhere the rule of the white man is dying.

5 D. Lowenthal, op. cit., p 789.

6 M. G. Smith, *The Plural Society in the British West Indies*, California, 1965. The author, a West Indian, has a penetrating analysis of West Indian culture in the first chapter of this book.

7 M. G. Smith, op. cit., p 7.

8 'The West Indians had to be helped to re-discover their own soil, their roots in it, to re-discover themselves. . . . The task was accepted by a pleiad of intellectuals, some of them coloured West Indian – like the Haitians Price Mars, Jacques Roumain, Milo Rigaud and the Cuban Nicolas Guillen – others white – like Melville Herskovits, Michel Seiris, Alfred Metraux and the Cuban Emilio Ballagas' . . . D. Guerin, *The West Indies and their Future*, London, 1961, p 93.

9 V. S. Naipaul in *The Middle Passage*, London, 1962, gives a caustic analysis of the effect of colonial rule on Trinidad society.

10 See G. Cumper, 'Labour Demand and Supply in the Jamaican Sugar Industry 1830–1950', *Social and Economic Studies*, vol 2, no 4, Kingston, 1954.

11 'The early historians of the present British islands in the West Indies were not English, or Scots or Irishmen. For the first colonizers of the Caribbean area were Spaniards' . . . *A Study on the Historiography of the British West Indies*, Mexico, 1956. In the Introduction of this study a West Indian historian, Dr Elsa Goveia, comments on the work of these first writers on the West Indies: Colon, who 'chronicled the tremendous achievement of a venerable father'; Peter Martyr, author of *De Orbe Nove*; Oviedo's *La historia general de las Indias*, the most famous of all the early Spanish histories of the Indies; Herrera his later successor; and Las Casas, whose *Brevissima Relacion de la destruycion de las Indias* and *Historia de las Indias* are 'the expression of a man of very great humanity, involved in the conflict that arose out of the historic colonizing movement which he . . . helped to preserve for the knowledge of a later day'.

These early histories were brought to the knowledge of the present-day West Indian public, and to some extent put within its reach, by one of the pioneers in the writing of West Indian history from the viewpoint of the Caribbean, Dr Eric Williams, in *Documents of West Indian History*, vol 1, 1492–1655, Trinidad, 1963. The purpose of the work is 'the cultural integration of the entire area, a synthesis of existing knowledge as the essential foundation of the great need of our time, closer collaboration among the various countries of the Caribbean with their common heritage of subordination and dictation by outside interests'.

Many of the references in this chapter are to historians whose work is represented in this collection of documents. Others are to another remarkable pioneer study, *Cuban Counterpoint*, by Fernando Ortiz, New York, 1947.

12, 13 E. Williams, op. cit., pp 17, 69, 32–3.

14 F. Ortiz, op. cit., p 272.

15 E. Williams, op. cit., pp 22–3.

16, 17 F. Ortiz, op. cit., pp 254–67.

18, 19, 20 F. Ortiz, op. cit., pp 268–82.

21–5 E. Williams, op. cit., pp 142, 143, 208.

3 AN ISLAND IS A WORLD

26 The West Indian 'diversity of history and character has inevitably affected their architecture'. In a *First Study of Georgian Buildings in the West Indies*, published under the title *Treasure in the Caribbean*, London, 1949, A. W.

Acworth refers to the eighteenth-century activity in building in the West Indies, the colonists adopting English architectural forms, and it was fortunate that this was the heyday of Georgian architecture. Examples are 'the finest group of buildings' in Jamaica in King's Square, Spanish Town; Clarence House in Antigua; and a group of Georgian buildings in Grenada, in St George's, 'the prettiest town in the British West Indies. No small part of its charm lies in the fact that red fish-scale tiles from Martinique are used to roof the houses instead of the shingles customary elsewhere.'

27 M. G. Smith, op. cit., p 4.

28 J. H. Parry and P. M. Sherlock, *Short History of the West Indies*, London, 1956, Chapter XIV: 'Patterns of Colonial Government'. Note also V. T. Harlow, *Barbados, 1625-1685*, Oxford, 1926, with its account of early local government in the island in Appendix A.

29 E. Williams, 'Four Poets of the Greater Antilles', *Caribbean Quarterly*, vol 2, no 4, Trinidad, pp 8-15.

30 The closed-circuit system of trade between colony and metropolitan power as it affected the Caribbean, especially Trinidad, is discussed by E. Williams in *History of the People of Trinidad and Tobago*, Trinidad, 1962, Chapter III: 'The Bankruptcy of Spanish Colonialism'.

31-3 C. Bosanquet, *A Letter to W. Manning Esq., M.P., on the Causes of the Rapid and Progressive Depreciation of West Indian Property*; bound with T. D. Selkirk, *A Letter to the Peers of Scotland*, London, 1807.

34 For a discussion of the trade relationships between the sugar islands, the North American colonies and Britain, and of the place of the islands 'in the imperial scheme of the eighteenth century' see E. Williams, *Capitalism and Slavery*, Chapel Hill, 1944, Chapter VI: 'The American Revolution'. There is an account of the West Indies–North American trade in R. Pares, *Yankees and Creoles*, London, 1956.

4 AFRICA IN FORCE

35 The best demographic study of the West Indies is by G. Roberts, *The Population of Jamaica, an analysis of its structure and growth*, Cambridge, 1957. It includes a section on population growth in the period of early slavery, and for this draws heavily on F. W. Pitman, *The Development of the British West Indies*, New Haven, 1917.

Changes in the number and structure of the West Indian population in the following period are dealt with by L. Ragatz, *Fall of the Planter Class in the Caribbean*, Washington, 1928.

Basic works for the seventeenth and eighteenth centuries are: J. B. du Tertre, *Histoire Generale des Antilles*, of which 2 vols were published in Paris in 1667, and a third in 1671; E. Ligon who gives a vivid first-hand account of the introduction of the sugar plantation into Barbados in *A True and Exact History of the Island of Barbados*, London, 1657; C. Leslie *A New History of Jamaica* . . . , London, 1740; B. Edwards, *The History, Civil and Commercial, of the British Colonies in the West Indies*, London, 1794; E. Long, *History of Jamaica*, 3 vols., London, 1774. Among recent works, R. Pares, *A West India Fortune*, London, 1950, is a history of a sugar plantation in Nevis and of the business of a sugar-factor in Bristol from 1685–1817: 'How Azariah Pinney landed in Nevis with £15 in his pocket', and of how his descendant John Pinney came to be worth 'about £267,000 – on paper'.

36 Census of 1960.

37 V. T. Harlow, op. cit., p 309.

38–9 For a recent discussion of the Slave-Population (the Exporting Countries, and Imports into the West Indies) see R. B. Le Page and D. De Camp, *Jamaican Creole*, London, 1960.

40 S. Mintz, 'Labour and Sugar in Puerto Rico and in Jamaica, 1800–50, *Comparative Studies in Society and History*, vol 1, no 3, March, 1959.

41 Census, op. cit.

42 See F. W. Pitman, op. cit.

43–6 See J. C. Hotten, *The Original Sailing Lists of Persons of Quality, emigrants* . . . New York, 1931. Also J. C. Jeaffreson, *A Young Squire of the Seventeenth Century*, London, 1878. For French Colonists: H. I. Priestley, *France Overseas through the Old Regime*, New York, 1939.

47 R. Hakluyt, *Divers Voyages Touching the Discovery of America*, London 1582. (The dedicatory preface reprinted by E. Taylor, 'Original Writings . . . of the two Richard Hakluyts'.)

48 George Chapman, Ben Jonson and John Marston satirise the travellers returning from across the Atlantic with tales of wonder, in *Eastward Ho*, London, 1605.

49 R. Hakluyt, op. cit., in the dedication to Philip Sidney.

50 C. Jeaffreson, op. cit., pp 259–60.

51 H. Whistler (see C. H. Firth, ed., the *Narrative of General Venables*, London, 1900).

52 R. Venables, supra.

53 C. Jeaffreson, op. cit., pp 124–8.

54 J. Macpherson, *Caribbean Lands*, London, 1963.

55 F. W. Pitman, op. cit.

56 For a valuable account of the Slave Trade, as operated by an English joint-stock corporation, see K. G. Davies, *The Royal African Company*, London, 1957.

5 WAR AND TRADE: 1650–1834

57 Thomas Lynch, who replaced Henry Morgan as Governor of Jamaica in 1671.

58 Malachi Postlethwayt explained and defended the mercantile policy and the Sugar and Slave Trades in three works: *Great Britain's Commercial Interest Explained and Improved* London 1757, *The African Trade, the Great Pillar and support of the British Plantation Trade*, London, 1745 and *The National and Private Advantages of the African Trade Considered*, London, 1746.

59 C.S.P.; Col. Ser.; Amer. and W.I., No. 849, 25 June 1702.

60–1 R. Pares gives a vivid picture of early colonial life in the Leeward Islands in *West India Fortune*, London, 1950. For a brief account see G. C. Merrill, *The Historical Geography of St Kitts and Nevis*, Mexico, 1958, Chapter IV.

62 W. J. Gardner, *History of Jamaica*, London, 1909, Period III, Chapter 2.

63 In December 1774 the Jamaica Assembly passed a petition expressing loyalty and rejecting as unconstitutional Parliament's claim to legislate for the colonies.

64 L. Ragatz, op. cit., pp 181–2.

65 The process was repeated in each sugar island: the opening up of virgin land, gutting of the land, and a fall in production. See E. Williams, *Capitalism and Slavery*, p 7.

66 L. Ragatz, op. cit., pp 209–213.

67 E. Williams, *History of the People of Trinidad and Tobago*, Trinidad, 1962, Chapter 3.

68 For an account of African immigration into Trinidad, see E. Williams, op. cit., Chapter 4.

69 H. T. Manning, *British Colonial Government after the American Revolution*, Newhaven, 1933, Chapters 11, 12.

6 A RACE SET FREE

70 The significance of 1938 for the labouring people of the West Indies is discussed by W. A. Lewis, *Labour in the West Indies*, London, 1939.

71 Writing of conditions in Trinidad in 1848, the Governor, Lord Harris said: 'a race has been freed, but a society has not been formed'.

72 M. G. Smith, op. cit., p 112.

73 E. Long, op. cit.

74 J. H. Parry, 'The Patent Offices in the British West Indies', *English Historical Review*, April, 1954, indicates the many abuses in the system.

75 James Stephen, who was given the task of drafting, almost overnight, a plan for emancipation that would give freedom to the slaves yet ensure that the plantations had the labour they needed. His solution was a system of compulsory labour as 'apprenticeship'. Goveia comments: 'The apprentice' ship was based on coercion, as slavery was. In principle, therefore, it was the last phase of slavery rather than the first instalment of freedom'.

76 M. G. Smith, op. cit., pp 107–8.

77 A. W. Acworth, *Treasure in the Caribbean*, London, 1949.

78 C. P. Lucas, *Historical Geography of the West Indies*, Oxford, 1905, pp 63–70.

79 Compare P. Curtin, *Two Jamaicas*, Boston, 1955. Chapters 2–4.

80 C. P. Lucas, op. cit., pp 68–9.

81 M. G. Smith, *The Plural Society of the British West Indies*, California, 1965, Chapter 5.

82 M. G. Smith, op. cit. Also see D. Hall 'Slaves and Slavery in the British West Indies', *Social and Economic Studies*, vol 2, no 4, Dec. 1962.

83 R. Pares, *West India Fortune*, London, 1950.

84 D. Hall, supra, p 308.

85–7 M. G. Smith, in Chapter 6 of *The Plural Society of the West Indies*, analyses the effects of Slavery and Emancipation in two Societies 'which formerly had this institution in common, but were otherwise dissimilar'; Jamaica and Zaria. Whereas in Zaria religion and law governed the relationships between masters and slaves, 'in Protestant slave-colonies care was taken to insulate the slaves against the incompatible influence of Christianity . . .'

7 THE CROWN IN CONTROL: 1834–1944

88 W. L. Mathieson, *British Slavery and its Abolition, 1822–38*, London, 1936.

89 D. Hall, *Free Jamaica*, New Haven, 1959.

90 See Chapter 7 in E. Williams, *History of the People of Trinidad and Tobago*, Trinidad, 1962.

91 P. Curtin, op. cit.

92–5 E. Williams, op. cit.

96 The Masters and Servants Act of 1840, Barbados. G. Lamming's *In the Castle of My Skin*, London, 1953, written a century later depicts a society still deeply marked by this experience.

97 See despatch from the Governor of Jamaica, Lord Metcalfe, to the Colonial office, no 50, March 1840, referred to by D. Hall in his excellent account of the period: *Free Jamaica*, New Haven, 1959.

98 See E. Williams, *History of the People of Trinidad and Tobago*.

99 S. Olivier, *Myth of Governor Eyre*, London, 1933. Morant Bay, where the rising occurred, is now a place of pilgrimage for Jamaican nationalists. Outside the Court House, where martial law was proclaimed, stands a statue of Paul Bogle, cast in black cement fondue, by Edna Manley. Reid's powerful novel *New Day* links the Morant Bay rising with 1938 and the national movement.

100 Robert Osborn; Jamaica House of Assembly, Debates XII, 48.

101 T. Milner, *The Present and Future State of Jamaica Considered*, London, 1839.

102 G. Roberts, op. cit., p 40.

103–5 M. Kerr, *Personality and Conflict in Jamaica*, Liverpool, 1952. Compare the discussion on colour in F. Henriques, *Family and Colour in Jamaica*, London, 1953.

106 M. Garvey, *Philosophy and Opinions*, New York, 1926, p 26. Garvey has been named as one of the national heroes of Jamaica, and his tomb in the George VI Memorial Park is a national shrine.

8 FROM COLONY TO COUNTRY

107 E. Williams, op. cit.

108 Revivalist practices have an important part in Jamaican electioneering, each party making full use of party hymns and songs. These are the very opposite of the Trinidad calypso which destroys by ridicule and innuendo.

109 See J. H. Parry and P. M. Sherlock, *Short History of the West Indies*, London, 1956, Chapter 18.

110–11 E. Wallace, 'The West Indies Federation, Decline and Fall', *International Journal*, 1962.

112 S. Selvon, *An Island is a World*, London, 1955.

113 D. Lowenthal, op. cit., p 787.

114, 115, 116 K. E. Boulding, 'Social Dynamics in West Indian Society', *Social and Economic Studies*, vol. 10, no 1, Kingston, 1961.

9 SEARCH FOR SECURITY

117 'Yet that view of West Indian History is misleading which sees it only as reflected in the island's intercourse with Britain and the other metropolitan powers. From a relatively early stage the area contributed substantially

towards its own economic advancement.' G. Cumper, *The Economy of the West Indies*, Kingston, 1960.

118 G. Roberts, Ch. 2, *Economy of the West Indies* (ed. Cumper).

119 W. A. Lewis, *Industrial Development in the Caribbean*, Trinidad, 1950.

120 G. Roberts, *Population of Jamaica*, pp 158–64.

121 R. Glass and H. Pollins give a comprehensive account of West Indian migration to Britain in recent years in *Newcomers*, London, 1960. See also R. Davison, *West Indian Migrants*, Oxford, 1962.

122 V. S. Naipaul, *The Middle Passage*, London, 1962.

123 E. F. Nash, *Trading Problems of the British West Indies in the Economy of the West Indies*, Kingston, 1960.

124 P. Abrahams, *Jamaica, An Island Mosaic*, London, 1957.

125 Report of the Trinidad Industrial Development Corporation, Port-of-Spain, Trinidad.

126 The total number of tourists visiting Jamaica in 1965 was 316,604, a 12½ per cent increase over 1964, and the estimated total expenditure by visitors was £23·5 million. From figures supplied by the Jamaican Tourist Board, Kingston, Jamaica.

127 For a discussion of the strategy of economic development in Cuba see D. Seers, *Cuba, The Economic and Social Revolution*, Chapel Hill, 1964.

10 FAMILY, CHURCH AND SCHOOL

128 Illuminating studies of the West Indian family will be found in R. T. Smith, *The Negro Family in British Guiana*, London, 1956; E. Clark, *My Mother Who Fathered Me*, London, 1957.

129 See M. G. Smith *The Plural Society in the British West Indies*, California, 1965, for a comparison of concubinage in Zaria and the British West Indies, dissimilar save in having been slave-societies.

130 M. G. Smith, supra.

131 R. T. Smith, *The Negro Family in British Guiana*.

132 M. Klass, 'East and West Indian: Cultural Complexity in Trinidad'; *Annals of the New York Academy of Sciences*, vol 83, art. 5, New York, 1950.

133 G. Roberts and L. Brathwaite, 'Mating among East Indian and Non-Indian Women in Trinidad,' *Social and Economic Studies*, University of the West Indies, vol 11, no 3, Sept. 1962. Also, vol 13, no 3, Sept. 1964, see L. Davids, 'The East Indian Family Overseas'.

134 G. Roberts and L. Brathwaite, supra.

135 H. B. Green, 'Values of Negro and East Indian School Children in

Trinidad', *Social and Economic Studies*, University of the West Indies, vol 14, no 2, June 1965.

136 F. Cundall (ed.), *Lady Nugent's Journal*, London, 1906.

137 G. Simpson, *The Shango Cult in Trinidad*, San Juan, 1965.

138 See M. Herskovits, *Life in a Haitian Valley*, New York, 1937.

139 In 1960 M. G. Smith, R. Augier and R. Nettleford, described the history, recent developments and current organization of the Ras Tafari Movement. The Report was published by the Institute of Social and Economic Research, University of the West Indies, 1960.

140 Ibid.

141 S. Olivier, *Jamaica, the Blessed Isle*, London, 1937.

142 M. Kerr, *Personality and Conflict in Jamaica*, Liverpool, 1952.

143–4 G. Roberts and N. Abdullah, 'Some Observations on the Educational Position of the Caribbean, *Social and Economic Studies*, vol 14, no 1, March 1965.

II FOLKLORE AND CUSTOM

145 Two studies on the subject are F. Cassidy, *Jamaica Talk*, London, 1961; R. B. Le Page and D. De Camp, *Jamaican Creole*, London, 1960.

146 F. Cassidy, supra.

147 See B. Gradamosi and U. Beier, *Yoruba Poetry*, a special edition of 'Black Orpheus', Ministry of Education, Ibadan, Nigeria.

148 M. W. Beckwith has a comprehensive collection of Jamaican Proverbs in *Jamaica Folk Lore*, published by the American Folk Lore Society, New York, vol 21, 1928.

149 S. Olivier, supra.

150 See P. M. Sherlock, *West Indian Folk Tales*, Oxford, 1966.

151 G. Carmichael, *History of the West Indian Islands of Trinidad and Tobago*, London, 1961.

152 This is based on an excellent account, 'Pan', published by the Tourist Trade Development Board of Trinidad and Tobago.

153 See M. G. Smith, supra; and M. Herskovits, *Trinidad Village*, New York, 1947.

154 See G. E. Simpson, *Shango Cult in Trinidad*, Puerto Rico, 1965.

155 S. Morrisseau–Le–Roy, *Recolte*, Port–au–Prince, 1946.

12 WEST INDIAN THEMES

156 See the second edition of C. L. R. James, *Black Jacobins*, in which the Appendix is an Essay: 'From Toussaint l'Ouverture to Fidel Castro'.

157 See E. Williams, *History of the People of Trinidad and Tobago*; E. Goveia, *Historiography of the British West Indies*. West Indian historical writing is growing in body through the efforts of a younger generation of scholars, Goveia, Hall, Augier and others based on the University of the West Indies.

158 C. L. R. James, supra.

159 G. R. Coulthard treats the subject in Chapters 5, 6 of *Race and Colour in the Caribbean*, Oxford, 1962.

160 C. L. R. James, supra.

161 Ibid.

162 R. Nettleford, 'National identity and Attitudes to Race in Jamaica', *Race*, vol 7, no 1, London, July 1965.

163 V. Bell. Reproduced in a number of West Indian Anthologies, including *Independence Anthology of Jamaican Literature*, Jamaica, 1962.

164 Translated by G. R. Coulthard *Caribbean Quarterly*, vol 2, no 4.

165 J. Hearne, born in Canada 1926.

166 E. M. Roach, 'I am the Archipelago'; in A. J. Seymour (ed.), *Anthology of West Indian Poetry*, British Guiana, 1957.

167 N. G. Sylvain, born Port-au-Prince 1901; contemporary of Jacques Roumain, Emile Roumer, Thoby Marcellin, Jean Brierre, all distinguished Haitian intellectuals.

168 Vic Reid, born in Jamaica 1913.

169 E. Mittelholzer, born in Guyana 1909, died 1965.

170 G. Lamming, born in Barbados 1927.

171 S. Selvon, born in Trinidad 1923.

172 V. S. Naipaul, born in Trinidad 1932.

173 O. Patterson, born in Jamaica 1940.

174 See G. R. Coulthard, supra; also C. A. M. Hennessy, 'Roots of Cuban Nationalism', *International Affairs*, vol 39, no 3, July 1963.

175 See A. W Pearse, 'West Indian Themes', *Caribbean Quarterly*, vol 2, no 2.

Acknowledgements

For permission to reproduce photographs:

Anne Bolt, 35, 42, 44, 46, 49, 51, 58, 62, 65, 68, 70, 71, 72, 73; from R. Bridgens, *West India Scenery*, London, 1938, by courtesy of the Royal Commonwealth Society, 14, 18, 19, 20, 33; Camera Press Ltd, 16, 38, 39, 40, 48, 52, 64;

COUNTRY	POSITION	AREA sq. miles	POPULATION
JAMAICA	18·0°N 77·0°W	4,411	1,606,600
TRINIDAD AND TOBAGO	10·20°N 61·20°W	1,980	947,000
BARBADOS	13·10°N 59·30°W	166	232,100
LEEWARD ISLANDS		342	123,000
Antigua	17·5°N 61·45°W	108	53,000
St Kitts	17·18°N 62·40°W	68	38,300
Nevis	17·18°N 62·40°W	36	12,700
Anguilla	18·15°N 63·0°W	35	5,500
Montserrat	16·45°N 62·14°W	$32\frac{1}{2}$	12,200
Barbuda	17·35°N 61·46°W	$62\frac{1}{2}$	1,200
BRITISH VIRGIN ISLANDS	18·20°N 64·40°W	60	8,000
WINDWARD ISLANDS		791	314,900
Dominica	15·30°N 61·20°W	305	60,000
Grenada	12·10°N 61·40°W	120	88,700
Grenadines		35	13,500
St Lucia	14·06°N 61·04°W	233	86,200
St Vincent	13·15°N 61·15°W	133	80,000
CAYMAN ISLANDS	19·16°N 81·20°W	100	7,600
TURKS ISLANDS	21·20°N 71·10°W	169	5,700

FACT SHEET

DENSITY per sq. mile	CAPITAL	PRINCIPAL EXPORTS
364	Kingston	Bauxite, Sugar, Bananas, Citrus
427	Port-of-Spain	Oil, Asphalt, Sugar, Citrus
1,398	Bridgetown	Sugar, Rum
494	St Johns	Sugar, Cotton
563	Basseterre	Sugar
355	Charlestown	Cotton
160		Cotton
375	Plymouth	Cotton
20		Cotton
	Roadtown	
197	Roseau	Bananas, Citrus
739	St Georges	Bananas, Nutmegs
370	Castries	Bananas, Coconuts
601	Kingstown	Bananas, Arrowroot
	Georgetown	
	Grand Turk	

Background to the Islands

JAMAICA has a total land area of 4,411 square miles. The two main products are sugar and bauxite. Sugar is the largest employer, giving occupation to about 80,000 people. Tourism has been developed with great success in recent years, the estimated earnings from this industry in 1965 being £25 million. The Government of Jamaica has given priority to economic development and over the period 1959 to 1963 the Gross Domestic Product at factor cost increased from £198·2 million to £254 million. The islands overseas trade in 1964 was made up of £100·7 million in imports and £78·8 million in exports. The imports consist largely of manufactured goods, machinery and transport equipment, food and chemicals. The exports are bauxite and alumina, sugar, bananas, clothing, rum, pimento and tobacco. In 1964 the United States supplied 30 per cent of Jamaica's imports, the United Kingdom 25 per cent, Canada 10 per cent and others 33 per cent. The United States took 35 per cent of the exports, United Kingdom 28 per cent, Canada 21 per cent and others 14 per cent.

TRINIDAD AND TOBAGO have an area of 1,980 square miles, Trinidad by itself having an area of 1,864 square miles and Tobago 116 square miles. The population is 947,000 (1960). Of this number 43·5 per cent is of African descent and 36·5 per cent of Indian descent (East Indians). Most of the wealth of Trinidad comes from its oil and asphalt. In 1963 the oil industry contributed 32 per cent to fiscal revenue. The rapid increase in population has produced an employment problem. In 1964 the island produced 50 million barrels of crude petroleum. In addition it imported very large quantities of crude oil from Venezuela and Saudi Arabia for its refineries. Sugar is the chief agricultural crop. The island's principal imports are crude petroleum, foodstuffs and machinery and its chief exports are refined petroleum products, crude and partly refined petroleum and sugar. It obtains 22 per cent of its total imports from Venezuela, 18 per cent from the United Kingdom, 18 per cent from

Saudi Arabia and 41 per cent from other sources. It sends 27 per cent of its exports to the United States, 21 per cent to the United Kingdom, 9 per cent to the Netherlands and its possessions, and 41 per cent to other sources.

Regional Organizations

It is very likely that both Jamaica and Trinidad and Tobago will become members of the Organization of American States. They are members of the United Nations and its associated organizations, and through membership in the British Commonwealth they benefit from the Commonwealth system of preferences.

BARBADOS is a crowded busy island. Sugar is the chief crop, production in 1964 reached 161,499 tons. Tourism is a major industry, the island having attractive beaches and a large number of good hotels. The educational system is one of the most comprehensive in the West Indies and the rate of illiteracy, 7 per cent, one of the lowest in the world. The chief exports are sugar, rum and molasses. About 50 per cent of the island's products go to the United Kingdom, 10 per cent to the United States, 7 per cent to Canada and 12 per cent to other Commonwealth countries. Barbados buys 30 per cent of its imports from Britain, 13 per cent from the United States, and 11 per cent from Canada.

THE LEEWARD ISLANDS. Consist of a group of islands in the northeast of the Caribbean Sea with a total area of 342 square miles. They are Antigua, Barbuda and Redonda which form one unit; St Christopher, often referred to as St Kitts, Nevis and Anguilla, which make up another unit; and Montserrat. The group is a scattered one, the more heavily populated islands lying between 63° and 64.30° west and 16.30° and 17.30° north.

ANTIGUA suffers from periodic droughts. The rainfall is barely sufficient for sugar cultivation. Cottonseed oil and meal are produced, and a cement factory and oil refinery are under construction. Tourism is an expanding industry. Sugar production averages just over 22,000 tons a year, but the industry has experienced many difficulties in recent years. The pattern of trade distribution shows about 30 per cent of the imports were from the United Kingdom, 25 per cent from the United States, 14 per cent from the West Indies. The United Kingdom takes 75–80 per cent of exports.

ST KITTS has an economy that is dominated by sugar. In contrast Nevis has little sugar; sea island cotton and coconuts are cultivated there, and small quantities of cotton in Anguilla. Basseterre has an entrepôt trade with the neighbouring Dutch and French islands.

In 1963 sugar production was 40,000 tons. The distribution of trade is of the order of 33 per cent imports from the United Kingdom, 30 per cent from the West Indies and Guyana, 15 per cent from Canada and from the United States respectively. About 50 per cent of exports go to the United Kingdom and to Canada.

MONTSERRAT lies about 27 miles southwest of Antigua, and is clearly visible from that island. About 7,000 acres are cultivated. Vegetables are grown in some quantity, especially carrots and tomatoes, and enough cattle are raised to meet the local needs. Sea Island cotton was for long the mainstay of the island. There are cotton ginneries and a lime-juice plant. Tourism has grown in importance in recent years, a number of North Americans having retired to the island.

BRITISH VIRGIN ISLANDS. Traditional occupations are fishing, stock raising and working in the United States Virgin Islands. The tourist industry is rapidly becoming an important source of income, because the islands are of enchanting beauty, and offer an escape from the rush of modern living.

THE WINDWARD ISLANDS. Consist of Grenada, St Lucia, St Vincent, Dominica, and a group of small islands known as the Grenadines. The islands lie almost on the same longitude, and within 12° and 16° north, Dominica being the most northerly, Grenada the most southerly. St Vincent is about 100 miles west of Barbados, and Grenada about the same distance north of Trinidad.

DOMINICA is larger than any of the other islands in the group. The chief crops are bananas, oranges, grapefruit and limes, coconuts, straw goods and copra. In 1963 imports amounted to 31 per cent from the United Kingdom, 18 per cent from the West Indies and 15 per cent from Canada. The United Kingdom buys 80–85 per cent of the products, and the West Indies 8 per cent.

GRENADA is linked for administrative purposes to Carriacou, the largest of the Grenadines. The chief export crops are cocoa, nutmegs and mace and bananas. The United Kingdom is the chief customer, taking about 32 per cent of the island's exports and sending to it 30–33 per cent of its imports. Grenada imports about 20 per cent of goods from the West Indies and about 15 per cent from the United States. It sends 13 per cent of its products to the United States, 11 per cent to West Germany and 26 per cent to other countries.

ST LUCIA has an area of 233 square miles. Like the other islands in the group it is very mountainous. In recent years bananas have become the main crop, followed by copra, cocoa and spices. Tourism is rapidly becoming one of the island's main industries. About 33 per cent of St Lucia's imports are from the

United Kingdom, 13 per cent from the United States and 12 per cent from Canada. Of the exports by far the largest proportion, about 80 per cent, goes to the United Kingdom and 15 per cent to two West Indian countries, Barbados and Trinidad and Tobago.

ST VINCENT is linked with the most northerly of the Grenadine islands, the total area of the whole unit being 152 square miles. Arrowroot was formerly the chief export crop, but it has been displaced by bananas. Sea Island cotton is another product, but production fluctuates because of the uncertainty regarding prices. The United Kingdom imports about 50 per cent of the island's products and sells to it about 30 per cent of its imports. The other most important trading partners are the United States, which sells about 12 per cent of the total goods imported into St Vincent and takes just under 20 per cent of its exports, and Trinidad and Tobago and Barbados. The principal imports, as with most of the islands, are food, chemicals, manufactured goods, machinery and transport equipment.

Select Bibliography

HISTORIOGRAPHY AND COLLECTIONS OF DOCUMENTS

Bell, K.N., and Morrell, W.P. (eds.), *Select Documents on British Colonial Policy (1830–60)*, Oxford, 1928

Donnan, E., *Documents Illustrative of the History of the Slave Trade to America*, Washington, 1930–5

Goveia, E., *A Study on the Historiography of the British West Indies to the end of the Nineteenth Century*, Mexico, 1956

Pressoir, C., Trouillot, E., and Trouillot, H., *Historiographie d'Haiti*, Mexico, 1953

Wilgus, C., *Histories and Historians of Hispanic America*, New York, 1942

Williams, E., *Documents of West Indian History, 1492–1655*, Port-of-Spain, 1963

Williams, E., *The British West Indies at Westminster, Part I, 1789–1832*, Trinidad, 1954

DISCOVERY AND SETTLEMENT (1492–1650)

Bullbrook, J.A., *The Aborigines of Trinidad*, Royal Victoria Institute Museum, Trinidad, 1960

Columbus, C. (trs. C. Jane), *The Journal of Christopher Columbus*, London, 1960

Cundall, F., and Sherlock, P.M., *The Aborigines of Jamaica*, Institute of Jamaica, Kingston, 1939

Hakluyt, R., *The Principal Navigations, Voyages, Traffiques and Discoveries of the English Nation (1589)*, 12 vols, Glasgow, 1903–5

Haring, C.H., *The Spanish Empire in America*, New York, 1947

Loven, S., *Origins of the Tainan Culture*, Goteborg, 1935

Morison, S.E., *Admiral of the Ocean Sea*, Boston, 1942

194

Morison, S.E., *Christopher Columbus, Mariner*, London, 1956
Newton, A.P., *The European Nations in the West Indies*, London, 1933
Oviedo y Valdes, G.F. de, *Historia General y Natural de las Indias*, 19 books, Sevilla, 1535

THE SETTLEMENT OF THE OUTER ISLANDS

Andrews, C.M., *The Colonial Period of American History*, 4 vols, New Haven, 1934-8
Du Tertre, J.B., *Histoire Generale des Antilles Habitées par les Francais*, 3 vols, Paris, 1667-71
Harlow, V.T., *History of Barbados 1625-85*, Oxford, 1926
Higham, C.S.S., *The Development of the Leeward Islands under the Restoration*, Cambridge, 1920
Morales Padron, F., *Jamaica Espanola*, Sevilla, 1952

THE PERIOD OF SLAVE-AND-SUGAR PLANTATIONS (1650–1834)

Beer, G.L., *British Colonial Policy 1754-65*, New York, 1907
Davidson, B., *Black Mother*, London, 1961
Edwards, B., *The History, Civil and Commercial, of the British Colonies in the West Indies*, London, 1794 (many editions)
Fortescue, Sir J.W., *History of the British Army*, 13 vols, London, 1899–1930
Herskovits, M.J., *Myth of the Negro Past*, New York, 1941
James, C.L.R., *Black Jacobins* (rev. edition), New York, 1963
Joseph, E.L., *History of Trinidad*, Trinidad, 1838
La Vaissiere, P., *Saint-Domingue 1629-1789*, Paris, 1909
Leslie, C., *A New History of Jamaica from the Earliest Accounts to the taking of Porto Bello . . .*, London, 1740
Leyburn, J.G., *The Haitian People*, New Haven, 1941
Ligon, E., *A True and Exact Study of the Island of Barbados*, London, 1657
Long, E., *History of Jamaica*, 3 vols, London, 1774
Manning, H.T., *British Colonial Government after the American Revolution*, New Haven, 1933
Mannix, D.P., and Cowley, M., *Black Cargoes*, London, 1962
Martin, G., *Histoire de l'Esclavage dans les Colonies Françaises*, Paris, 1948
Morales, Carrion, A., *Puerto Rico and the Non-Hispanic Caribbean*, Rio Piedras, 1952
Pares, R., *War and Trade in the West Indies, 1739-63*, Oxford, 1936
Pares, R., *A West India Fortune*, London, 1950

Pares, R., *Yankees and Creoles*, London, 1956
Pitman, F.W., *The Development of the British West Indies, 1700–1763*, New Haven, 1917
Poyer, J., *History of Barbados*, London, 1808
Ragatz, L.J., *The Fall of the Planter Class in the Caribbean*, Washington, D.C., 1928
Raynal, G.T.F., *Histoire Philosophique et Politique des Establissements et du Commerce des Europeens dans les Deux Indes*, first edition in English, 4 vols, London, 1776
Southey, T., *Chronological History of the West Indies*, 3 vols, London, 1827
Sypher, W., *Guinea's Captive Kings*, Chapel Hill, 1942
Williams, E., *Capitalism and Slavery*, Chapel Hill, 1944
Wyndham, H.A., *The Atlantic and Slavery*, Oxford, 1935

FROM SLAVERY TO FREEDOM (1800–1840)

Burn, W.L., *Emancipation and Apprenticeship in the British West Indies*, London, 1937
Clarkson, T., *The History of the Rise, Progress and Accomplishment of the Abolition of the African Slave Trade*, 2 vols, London, 1808
Davy, J., *The West Indies before and after Slave Emancipation*, London, 1854
Du Bois, W.E.B., *The Suppression of the Slave Trade*, Cambridge, Mass., 1896
Mathieson, W.L., *British Slavery and its Abolition 1823–38*, London, 1926
Mathieson, W.L., *British Slave Emancipation 1838–49*, London, 1932
Schoelcher, Y., and Cesaire, A. (eds.), *Esclavage et Colonisation*, Paris, 1948
Sewell, W., *The Ordeal of Free Labour in the West Indies*, New York, 1861

FROM COLONY TO COUNTRY (1860–1938)

Blanshard, P., *Democracy and Empire in the Caribbean*, New York, 1952
Cumpston, I.M., *Indians Overseas in British Territories, 1835–65*, Oxford, 1953
Curtin, P.D., *Two Jamaicas, 1830–65*, Harvard, 1955
Hall, D., *Free Jamaica 1838–1865*, New Haven, 1959
Kepner, C.D., and Soothill, J.H., *The Banana Empire*, New York, 1935
Mathieson, W.L., *The Sugar Colonies and Governor Eyre, 1849–66*, London, 1936
MacMillan, W.M., *Warning from the West Indies*, London, 1938
Nath, D., *A History of Indians in British Guiana*, London, 1950
Olivier, Sir S., *The Myth of Governor Eyre*, London, 1933

Olivier, Sir S., *Jamaica, the Blessed Isle*, London, 1937
Simey, T.S., *Welfare and Planning in the West Indies*, Oxford, 1946
Williams, E., *The Negro in the Caribbean*, New York, 1942
Wrong, H., *Government of the West Indies*, Oxford, 1923

GENERAL

History

Benians, E.A., Holland Rose, J., and Newton, A.P. (eds.), *The Growth of the New Empire, 1783–1870*, Cambridge, 1940
Burns, A., *The History of the British West Indies*, London, 1954
Burn, W.L., *The British West Indies*, London, 1951
Deer, N., *The History of Sugar*, 2 vols, London, 1949–50
Garcia, A., *History of the West Indies*, London, 1965
Lucas, C.P., *Historical Geography of the West Indies*, Oxford, 1905
Merrill, C.G., *The Historical Geography of St Kitts and Nevis*, Mexico, 1958
Parry, J.H., and Sherlock, P.M., *Short History of the West Indies*, London, 1956
Revert, E., *Les Antilles*, Paris, 1954
Saco, J.A., *Historia de la Esclavitud de la Raza Africana en el Nuevo Mundo*, 4 vols, Havana, 1938

Sociology, Economics, Politics

Abrahams, P., *Jamaica*, London, 1957
Bell, W., *Jamaican Leaders*, Berkeley, 1964
Carley, M., *Jamaica, the Old and the New*, London, 1963
Clarke, E., *My Mother who Fathered Me*, London, 1957
Edwards, D., *An Economic Study of Small Farming in Jamaica*, University of the West Indies, 1961
Guerin, D., *The West Indies and their Future*, London, 1961
Henriques, F.M., *Family and Colour in Jamaica*, London, 1953
Herskovits, M.J., *Trinidad Village*, New York, 1947
Kerr, M., *Personality and Conflict in Jamaica*, Liverpool, 1952
Lewis, A.W., *Labour in the West Indies*, London, 1939
Roberts, G., *The Population of Jamaica*, Cambridge, 1957
Simpson, G., *The Shango Cult in Trinidad*, San Juan, 1965
Smith, M.G., *The Plural Society of the British West Indies*, California, 1965
Smith, M.G., *Kinship and Community in Carriacou*, Newhaven, 1962

197

Literature, Language, Travel

Campbell, G., *First Poems*, Kingston, 1945

Cassidy, F.G., *Jamaica Talk*, London, 1961

Cesaire, A., *Cahier d'un Retour au pays natal*, Paris, 1947

Coulthard, G., *Race and Colour in the Caribbean*, Oxford, 1962

Garvey, M. (ed., Jacques-Harvey, A.), *Philosophy and Opinions of Marcus Garvey*, 2 vols, New York, 1923

Hearne, J., *Stranger at the Gate*, London, 1956; *The Faces of Love*, London, 1959; *Autumn Equinox*, London, 1959; *Land of the Living*, London, 1961

James, C.L.R., *Beyond a Boundary*, London, 1963

Lamming, A., *In the Castle of My Skin*, London, 1953; *The Emigrants*, London, 1954; *The Pleasures of Exile*, London, 1960

Mittelholzer, E.A., *A Morning at the Office*, London, 1950

Naipaul, V.S., *Miguel Street*, London, 1959; *The Suffrage of Elvira*, London, 1958; *The Mystic Masseur*, London, 1957; *A House for Mr Biswas*, London, 1961; *The Middle Passage*, London, 1962

Pales Matos, L., *Poesia (1915–1956)*, San Juan, 1957

Price-Mars, J., *Ainsi parla l'oncle*, Port-au-Prince, 1928

Reid, V., *New Day*, New York, 1949

Selvon, S., *A Brighter Sun*, London, 1952; *Lonely Londoners*, London, 1956; *Ways of Sunlight*, London, 1957

Who's Who

ACCOMPONG (dates unknown). Maroon leader in the successful struggle against the English for independence in the period 1690–1738; brother of Cudjoe. A Jamaican country town is named after him.

ADAMS, Sir Grantley, b. 1898. Barbados lawyer and politician; educated Harrison College and Oxford; attacked oligarchic planter government in 1930s, and became leader of the Barbados Labour Party after riots in 1937; took part in reviving West Indian Labour Congress with Cipriani, 1944. Leader of the Barbados government; became Prime Minister of West Indies, 1958–62.

BAKER, Captain Lorenzo Dow (1826–68). American sea-captain, pioneered the banana export trade from Jamaica; a principal figure in the Boston Fruit Company later incorporated into the United Fruit Company.

BAKER, Moses (dates unknown). A freed slave brought to Jamaica in 1783 from the United States by a loyalist family. Laid the foundation of the native Baptist Churches in Jamaica. Partly as a result of his work the first Baptist missionary was sent to Jamaica in 1814.

BALBOA, Vasco Nunez de (1475–1517). Spanish explorer and conquistador. He was the first European to cross the isthmus of Panama and see the Pacific Ocean.

BENBOW, Vice-Admiral John (1653–1702). In command of a fleet based on Port Royal in 1702 at start of War of the Spanish Succession. Died as a result of wounds received in action against French fleet under du Casse. Buried in Kingston Parish Church.

BERRIO, Antonio de (dates unknown). Governor of Trinidad, 1592. Raleigh burnt his capital, St Joseph, and took de Berrio prisoner, seeking his help in the search for El Dorado.

BIRD, Vere, b. 1909. Founder and leader of the Antigua Labour Movement in 1937 and first Chief Minister of Antigua.

BLIGH, Captain William (1753–1817). Commanded HMS *Bounty* in expedition to the South Seas for food-crops (including the breadfruit) for the West Indies in 1787. In 1793 he brought large cargo of breadfruit trees and other economic plants to the West Indies.

BOGLE, Paul, d. 1865. Honoured as a national hero of Jamaica; deacon of native Baptist Church at Stony Gut near Morant Bay, Jamaica, in 1865; friend of George William Gordon; able, energetic leader with the masterful character of an African chief; led protest march to Morant Bay, 7 October 1865, which ended in riot. Arrested and hanged after summary military trial. A statue of Bogle erected in 1965 stands outside the Morant Bay Court House.

BOLIVAR, Simon (1783–1830). Leading figure in the liberation of the Spanish colonies in South and Central America; first President of Venezuela; often called the Washington of South America, but his campaigns were on a vaster scale and over a longer period.

BOUKMAN (dates unknown). A slave, said to have been born in Jamaica, leader of the rising of the Haitian slaves in 1790. This rising failed, but the scope and planning put Boukman among the architects of Haitian freedom.

BUSTAMANTE, Sir Alexander, b. 1884 as Alexander Clarke in Jamaica, son of an Irish planter and part-Indian mother; spent his youth in Spain. He took the name of Bustamante, a Spanish sea-captain who befriended him. After working in the United States he returned to Jamaica in 1932; emerged as labour leader after the riots in 1938. Detained for 17 months during war but retained hold on mass of Jamaican people. Founder of Jamaica Labour Party, and founder and life-President of Bustamante Industrial Trade Union. First Chief Minister of Jamaica (1944–54) and appointed first Prime Minister in 1962.

BUTLER, Uriah (dates unknown). A Grenadian, who migrated to the Trinidad oilfields and emerged as leader of Trinidad workers during the riots of 1938. Later a member of the Trinidad Legislative Council.

BUXTON, Thomas Fowell (1786–1845). Son of Essex landowner; an evangelical like Wilberforce; brother-in-law of Elizabeth Fry; member of Parliament in 1818; leader in movement for abolition of slavery.

CHACON, Don Jose Maria (dates unknown). Termed by Williams as Trinidad's 'most distinguished governor . . . a man of no mean intellectual gifts and administrative ability'; reorganized administration of island; reformed system of land tenure; secured liberal treatment of slaves through Cedula of 1789; yielded Trinidad to greatly superior English forces in 1797.

CHRISTOPHE, Henri (1767–1820). A slave employed as waiter in an hotel at Cap Francois, Haiti; leader with Toussaint in Haitian War of Independence; became ruler of north on death of Dessalines in 1806, his rival the mulatto Petion ruling the south; built the massive citadel.

CLARKSON, Thomas (1760–1847). In 1785 won Cambridge Prize Essay for essay, 'Should the unwilling be given into slavery?' His research findings made him an ardent abolitionist; conducted skilled campaign of public enlightenment about evils of slavery.

CODRINGTON, Christopher (1668–1710). Governor-General of Leeward Islands. Bequeathed two estates, Cousett's and Codrington's with some slaves and cattle to the Society for the Propagation of the Gospel, to maintain a University College, teachers and students to be 'under the vows of poverty, chastity and obedience'. Codrington College is now a Theological Seminary affiliated with the University of the West Indies.

COLUMBUS, Christopher (1451–1506). Born in Genoa, son of a wool-weaver; moved to Lisbon, centre of exploration and colonization under Henry the Navigator (1394–1460); failed to win Portuguese support for a carefully planned attempt to find a western route to the Indies. Set out on his first voyage in 1492 from Palos with backing of Isabella and Ferdinand, Sovereigns of Spain; established permanent contact between Europe and America; made four transatlantic voyages (1492, 1494, 1498 and 1502).

CUDJOE (dates unknown). Best known of the Maroon leaders; with his brothers, Accompong and Johnny and sub-chiefs Quao and Cuffee, fought the First Maroon War in Jamaica; by treaty of 1783 won recognition of Maroon freedom and independence.

DE BOLAS, Juan (dates unknown). His name given to a range of hills in parish of St Catherine, Jamaica. Leader of band of free slaves who fought with Ysasi and Spaniards against English invaders in 1665, then in 1660 joined English. His knowledge of the country and of the hidden Spanish bases helped English to crush last Spanish resistance.

DE POINCY (dates unknown). Governor of St Christophe on behalf of Knights of Malta; in 1639 sent away the leading Huguenots to settle Tortuga as French outpost. This later became base for buccaneers.

D'ESNAMBUC, Pierre (dates unknown). Founder of French settlement in St Christophe (St Kitts), where he arrived in 1625.

DESSALINES, Jean Jacques (1758-1806). An African slave, one of Toussaints chief leaders in liberation of Haiti. In 1804 proclaimed himself Emperor of Haiti; restoring the island's early Taino name, Haiti, 'mountain land'. Ruled till 1806 when he was assassinated.

DRAKE, Sir Francis (c. 1540-96). A leading figure in the attack on Spain in the Caribbean, aimed at cutting the sinews of Spanish power; that is, the flow of silver and gold from Panama to Cadiz.

DU CASSE, Jean Baptiste (1646-1715). Of Huguenot parentage; highly success-ful privateer; promoted governor of St Domingue, 1691; invaded Jamaica in 1694 after destruction by earthquake of Port Royal; later, with de Pointis, sacked Cartagena.

DU TERTRE, Jean Baptiste (1610-87). Author of *Histoire Generale des Antilles Habitées par les Français*; drew on his personal knowledge of people and places in region (*see* Select Bibliography).

EDWARDS, Bryan (1743-1800). Jamaica planter, author of *The History, Civil and Commercial, of the British Colonies in the West Indies* (*see* Select Bibliography).

EYRE, Sir Edward (1815-1901). Appointed to Jamaica as acting Governor 1862; his alarmist tactics, brutal repression of the Morant Bay rising and hanging of George William Gordon in 1865, resulted in inquiry by Royal Commission and his recall. Persuaded the Jamaica House of Assembly to surrender its powers, and island became Crown Colony.

FEDON, Julien (dates unknown). Coloured Grenada planter, leader in 1795 of rebellion against English, instigated by French revolutionary agent Victor Hughes; subdued after three months' struggle; Fedon's camp in Grenada mountains preserves his memory.

FLEURY, Jean (dates unknown). French corsair in service of Jean d'Ango, Dieppe merchant, pioneered entry into Caribbean of French privateers. His capture of two Spanish treasure ships off Azores in 1523, containing loot taken by Cortes in Mexico, showed wealth to be obtained from attacks on Spanish Indies.

GAGE, Thomas (c. 1596–1656). Ex-Dominican priest, author of The English American, first-hand account of Spanish Indies; violent supporter of Cromwell's 'Western Design' which resulted in conquest of Jamaica, 1655. The contempt for Spanish forces in the Caribbean, which characterized the expedition, was due partly to his information.

GARVEY, Marcus (1887–1940). Jamaican national hero. Founded the Universal Negro Improvement Association in 1914; gained prominence as Negro leader in Harlem in period 1916–20; built up large organization and attracted international notice with his plans for a return to Africa. Sentenced to prison in the United States on charge of using the mails to defraud; later returned to Jamaica, where he continued his work. He died in London. Garvey's leadership and insistence on the dignity and equality of the black man led to radical changes in social attitudes in the West Indies.

GORDON, George William (c. 1820–65). Illegitimate son of white planter and slave woman; became landowner in St Thomas; magistrate and vestryman for the parish; devoted himself to advance of black Jamaicans as against white oligarchic planter rule in Vestry and central government; elected member of House of Assembly in 1850s and again in 1863; he incurred enmity of Governor Eyre for outspoken attacks on government abuses; court-martialled and hanged in 1865, at time of Morant Bay rising, by an act of judicial murder. Today he is commemorated in Gordon House, meeting place of Jamaica's parliament.

GRANT, Sir John Peter (1774–1848). First governor of Jamaica as Crown Colony (1866–74); reorganized judiciary, civil service, local government, established efficient police force and public services.

GUACANAGARI (dates unknown). Arawak cacique in Hispaniola who befriended Columbus on his arrival in 1492.

HAMILTON, Alexander (1757–1804). Born in Nevis, illegitimate son of Scots-man James Hamilton; brought up in St Croix, where his teacher soon recognized his unusual ability; sent to King's College, New York, and then entered on career as one of architects of the United States.

HATUEY (dates unknown). Arawak cacique, courageous leader of Arawak resistance to Spanish colonization in Cuba, in contrast with Guacanagari.

HAWKINS, Sir John (1532–95). Elizabethan naval commander, Vice-Admiral against Spanish Armada, co-leader with Drake of abortive expedition against Spanish Indies in 1555. Between 1562 and 1568 pioneered triangular trade based on sale of English goods in West Africa, African slaves in Caribbean, Caribbean sugar and other products in England.

HEYN, Piet (1578–1629). Brilliant Dutch commander whose naval victory and capture of Spanish treasure fleet at Matanzas Bay in Cuba (1627) seriously weakened Spain in the Caribbean.

HILL, Richard (1795–1872). Coloured Jamaican intellectual, associated with Jordon in struggle against civil disabilities; appointed one of special magistrates to safeguard rights of Negroes during apprenticeship period.

JORDON, Edward (1800–69). Coloured Jamaican, led movement for removal of civil disabilities from free coloured people in 1820s; editor of *The Watchman*.

KNIBB, William (1803–45). Went to Jamaica as Baptist missionary in 1825. He vigorously attacked slavery, was arrested in 1831 at time of the slave rising in St James; on his release went to England and campaigned actively for abolition. After emancipation pioneered with Thomas Burchell and James Phillippo in establishment of free villages.

LABAT, Jean Baptiste (1663–1738). Born in Paris; Dominican priest, sent to Martinique in 1693 and rose to be Superior; served in French islands for 13 years; author of *Nouveau Voyage aux Isles de l'Amerique* in 1724.

LAS CASAS, Bartolomé de (1474–1566). Dominican friar, went to Hispaniola in 1502 with Ovando's expedition; ardent champion of Indians against Spanish colonists; appointed Protector of the Indians. Author of *Historia de las Indias*.

LE CLERC, General Victor Emmanuel (1772–1802). Brother-in-law of Napoleon. Arrived in Caribbean in 1802 with fleet and 20,000 men to subdue Haiti, reintroduce slavery, and establish French Empire in America based on Louisiana. Captured Toussaint by trickery. Died in Haiti of yellow fever.

LE VASSEUR (1828–1911). A Huguenot, leader of French privateers in Tortuga, which he systematically fortified. Assassinated in 1653.

LISLE, George (dates unknown). A freed slave from the Bahamas who, with Moses Baker, founded native Baptist Churches in Jamaica at the end of the eighteenth century.

L'OLLONOIS, François (dates unknown). One of the most savage of the seven-teenth-century pirates of the period of Henry Morgan. His base was Tortuga.

MACEO (1845–96). A mulatto leader in the Cuban Ten Years War against Spain, with Maximo Gomez. Maceo was killed in 1896.

MARTI, Jose (1853–95). National hero of Cuba; son of Spanish sergeant who became captain of rural police. In exile in United States, 1880–95; he cease-lessly advocated Cuban independence; one of most magnetic and idealistic personalities in Caribbean history; rallied American support for Cuba; led revolt in Cuba in 1895 and was killed in one of the first skirmishes.

MANLEY, Norman Washington, b. 1893. Jamaican lawyer and politician; Rhodes Scholar; served in First World War, then completed legal studies; in period of 1938 riots took up cause of labour; worked at first with Bustamante, then broke with him. Founded People's National Movement; spearheaded economic development as Chief Minister (1954–62) and Premier. First Leader of Opposition in Parliament after independence (1962).

METCALFE, Sir Charles (1785–1846). Liberal-minded Governor of Jamaica (1839–42) in critical period following termination of apprenticeship.

MICO, Lady (dates unknown). The Mico Training College in Jamaica, partly supported by the Mico Trust, is named after Lady Mico who, in 1670, left

£1,000 for the redemption of poor Christian slaves in Barbary. The money accumulated, till in 1827 it amounted to £127,000. The Court of Chancery accepted a proposal by Buxton for using the money to promote education among the newly freed people of the West Indies.

MORGAN, Sir Henry (c. 1635–88). Indentured servant in Barbados, ran away to join buccaneers and became one of their leaders while in his twenties; sacked Cartagena, Porto Bello, Panama; in the 1660s–70s the uncrowned King of Port Royal; became Lieutenant-Governor of Jamaica.

MUNOZ MARIN, Luis, b. 1898. Puerto Rican politician and nationalist; son of nationalist Munoz Rivera; took his Popular Party to power in 1940, making the cause of the peasant, the jibaro, his own. Devised formula of Common- wealth of Puerto Rico in free association with the United States, by which Puerto Rico gets many advantages of statehood.

NELSON, Admiral Horatio (1758–1805). Served in Nevis, where he married Mrs Nisbett, Antigua and Jamaica, where Nelson's Quarter Deck at Port Royal is still preserved. Nursed back to health after illness contracted in Central American campaign by slave woman, Cuba Cornwallis, at Port Royal.

OGÉ, Jacques Vincent (1755–91). Haitian free mulatto, friend of Condorcet and Abbe Gregoire; leader of rising in Santo Domingo in 1790, with Chavannes, one of the mulattoes who had fought in the American War of Independence. Ogé and Chavannes were tortured and executed.

OLIVIER, Lord (1859–1943). Liberal colonial governor of Jamaica, 1907– 1913. Later Secretary of State for India in first Labour government in Britain.

OSBORN, Robert (1835–89). Associated with Edward Jordon and group of coloured men in Jamaica House of Assembly in period 1834–65; co-editor of *The Watchman*.

PÉTION, Alexandre Sabes (1770–1818). Mulatto leader in Haitian War of Independence; ruler of the south after death of Dessalines in 1807.

PICTON, Colonel Thomas (1758–1815). Governor of Trinidad after its conquest from Spain in 1797. Appointed civil governor in 1801.

PONCE DE LEON, Juan (1460–1521). Accompanied Columbus to Caribbean in 1493 as foot-soldier; founded San Juan de Puerto Rico and established island as Spanish colony.

REEVES, Conrad (1821–1902). First coloured man to become Chief Justice of Barbados. In 1877 resolutely opposed Colonial Office attempt to put two official members in House of Assembly.

RODNEY, Admiral (1719–92). Defeated de Grasse off The Saintes in 1781, saving Jamaica from invasion. Captured St Eustatius in 1781, gaining immense booty. Rodney's preoccupation with booty prejudiced England's position in North America.

SHARP, Granville (1735–1813). Engaged in public agitation against slave trade as result of contact with Joseph Strong, a slave in England who was cast adrift by his master because he was ill and useless. Later took up case of another slave, James Somerset, resulting in judgment by Lord Mansfield in June 1772 that in the absence of positive law on the subject the right of property in slaves could not be upheld before the courts in England. This judgment had the effect of liberating all held as slaves in England.

STOKES, Luke, d. 1657. Governor of Nevis, led a party of 1,800 persons in 1657 to Jamaica to settle. Many were wiped out by disease. Name survives in Stokes Hall.

TOUSSAINT LOUVERTURE, Dominique François (1743–1803). Like Bolivar and Washington took his country into independence, but he in addition took it from slavery into freedom; led Haitian rising from 1791 until 1802, when he was tricked by Le Clerc and sent to France; died in prison in 1803. His work was completed by Dessalines who declared Haiti independent in 1804.

WARNER, Thomas, d. 1648. Involved in Roger North's unsuccessful attempt to found a colony in Guiana in 1620; on return voyage to England he founded St Kitts in 1623, the first English colony in the Caribbean; was made Governor-General of the Caribbee Islands. Died in 1648. Tomb is in St Thomas Churchyard, St Kitts.

WILBERFORCE, William (1759–1833). Son of a Hull merchant, educated at Cambridge, entered Parliament 1780; from 1789 to 1807 actively advocated abolition of slave trade. He led the emancipation movement with Thomas Buxton.

WILLIAMS, Eric, b. 1911. Educated in Port-of-Spain and Oxford, from which he graduated B.A. in 1935. Professor of Political Science, Howard University; served with Caribbean Commission; founded the People's National Movement, 1956; first Chief Minister of Trinidad and Tobago. First Prime Minister of his country on its achieving independence in 1962. Historian, leader in the presentation of West Indian History from Caribbean point of view (*see* Select Bibliography).

WOODFORD, Sir Ralph (1784–1828). Governor of Trinidad, 1813–28. Able paternalistic administrator, concerned with land problem, immigration to meet Trinidad's labour shortage, and improvement of Port-of-Spain where his name survives in Woodford Square.

Index

213